George Tremlett has been a rock writer almost since the music began in the mid-Fifties. He left King Edward VI School, Stratford-upon-Avon, in 1957 and then spent four years on *The Coventry Evening Telegraph* writing their daily TV column and reviewing all the visiting pop package shows.

In 1961 he moved to London and became a freelance writer, working part-time for *The New Musical Express.* He has since been London correspondent for TV and pop magazines in Japan, Holland, Sweden, the United States, Belgium, Germany, Australia, New Zealand and Finland. In this he is partnered by his wife, Jane. They have also contributed to most major British teenage magazines.

Outside pop music journalism, George Tremlett pursues a political career as a member of the Greater London Council. For eleven years he was also a councillor in Richmond-upon-Thames.

AF469591

Also by George Tremlett

THE DAVID BOWIE STORY
THE OSMOND STORY
THE GARY GLITTER STORY
THE DAVID ESSEX STORY
THE ROLLING STONES STORY
THE MARC BOLAN STORY
THE WHO
THE SLADE STORY
THE PAUL McCARTNEY STORY

George Tremlett

The Cliff Richard Story

Futura Publications Limited

A Futura Book

First published in Great Britain in 1975
by Futura Publications Limited
Copyright © George Tremlett 1975

This book is sold subject to the condition that it shall not, by way of trade or otherwise, be lent, re-sold, hired out or otherwise circulated without the publisher's prior consent in any form of binding or cover other than that in which it is published and without a similar condition including this condition being imposed on the subsequent purchaser.
ISBN 0 8600 7232 0

Printed in Great Britain by
Hazell Watson & Viney Ltd
Aylesbury, Bucks

Futura Publications Limited
110B & C Warner Road
Camberwell, London SE5

ACKNOWLEDGEMENTS

It is now more than fifteen years since I wrote my first Cliff Richard news story. Since then I have interviewed him many times, often two or three times a year, and have kept records of all those discussions together with thick files of cuttings, press releases, invitations to film shows, movie photos, etc. It is upon this that I have based the chronology in the appendix, and the book itself is based on my own interviews with Cliff Richard, Hank Marvin, Bruce Welch, Jet Harris, Olivia Newton-John and others associated with him.

CHAPTER ONE

Cliff Richard has often been called, a little unkindly to my mind, the 'vicar of pop'. It is one of those supposedly clever-clever journalistic phrases that begins with one headline and a smirk on a sub-editor's cheek; is eyed enviously in a rival music paper office ('Wish I'd thought of that!'), and then repeated half-unconsciously by that paper a few weeks later, soon passing into everyday language. Once any performer has a tag like that, be he a comedian, musician, singer or actor, it becomes very hard to live down; very soon the phrase becomes an inseparable part of his image – without him changing in any way.

And so it was with Cliff Richard.

Mention his name to anyone interested in pop music, and it is not very likely that they will tell you how they remember seeing him at Butlin's holiday camp in 1958; nor will they mention that 'Move It' was Britain's first home-grown rock 'n' roll record, or that Cliff's backing group, The Shadows, were the original idols of most of today's world-renowned rock bands. No, they will joke perhaps about his Palladium appearances and seasons in cabaret at the Talk of the Town, mention how 'neat' he looks, and above all smile over that holy-holy image.

All of which does Cliff Richard a considerable injustice.

He really is one of the great originals of British rock 'n' roll, and has in his time been a major artist in nearly every country in the world with the exception of the United States, packing concert halls throughout Europe and Scandinavia, across Australia, New Zealand, Hong Kong, Singapore and Japan, and has long been one of the most successful artistes ever to visit South Africa and Rhodesia.

Since that first hit single in 1958, he has had over sixty chart entries in Britain alone; has twice come close to winning the Eurovision Song Contest; has starred in some of the most successful pop films ever made; has broken every box office record at the London Palladium; has been re-booked again and again to appear in cabaret at the Talk of the Town; has drawn considerable audience-ratings with successive thirteen-week BBC

TV series, and taken it all in his stride.

Together with Tommy Steele and Cilla Black, he is one of the few all-round entertainers to have been given an all-generation audience by pop music.

Since he first started talking publicly about his beliefs as a Christian in 1966, he has also become a figure of even wider importance. He has spent much of his time visiting schools, talking to students, sharing conference platforms with bishops and even Dr Billy Graham, making two religious films (and even donating the £40 wage that the actors' trade union Equity said he *had* to be paid to charity), and helping to run a church youth club in North London.

Personally, having discussed them with him on several occasions, I find his religious beliefs rather simplistic, but of his total sincerity I have no doubt at all. For he also possesses a genuine warmth of personality, is relatively modest in his life-style and has – more than most artistes – managed to make that transition from teenage idol to normal adult.

His way of life these days is simple, he shares a house in North London with religious teacher Bill Latham. It is a Georgian style house that he and Latham bought together and Bill's mother lives there with them, looking after the home, cooking their meals.

The house is within easy travelling distance of Cheshunt Secondary Modern School, which was where Cliff spent his schooldays after failing his 11-plus examination. Although much better at football and athletics than the more conventional school pursuits, he remains deeply attached to the school, and counts several of the younger teachers who have joined the staff since he was a pupil there among his closest friends. Bill Latham himself is now the religious teacher there and as well as sharing a home with Cliff he and other teachers like Graham Disbury have frequently spent holidays at Cliff's other home in the Portuguese fishing village of Albufeira, which he bought ten years ago, and which he often lends to his friends.

If the school has a money-raising function, Cliff will support it if he can. He frequently takes a swim in the school pool or plays tennis and badminton (though he also has his own tennis court behind his home and belongs to a badminton club in Finchley), and he also maintains close contact with his former

English and drama teacher, Miss Jay Norris.

'She has always taken an interest in me and in my career,' he once told me. 'If I hadn't gone into show business she would probably have guided me into something else.'

Cliff eventually left the school at the age of fifteen with only one pass in his General Certificate of Education examinations (significantly enough in English Language), but in the mid-Sixties he started studying Religious Instruction and gained another GCE pass in that, and more recently has been thinking of taking further examinations in English Literature and Mathematics, though he is less certain of leaving show business to become a teacher now that he has been able to combine his religious work with his schedule as an entertainer so successfully.

'I'm sorry now that I left school when I did because I'd like to have learned more than I did,' he told me, adding that he thought this gave one a good foundation for whatever career one chooses, though it could be said that he has since made up for any educational deficiences he might have had by becoming an avid reader and a much-travelled and aware person.

If his home and his former school and the relationships that combine the two are the foundations of his domestic life, the cornerstone is undoubtedly his Church. His work in television, the theatre, cabaret and his recording commitments are all so arranged that he always has the time to devote to this area of his life. 'I never accept any booking that means me having to be out of the country for more than two weeks at a time,' he says, explaining that he keeps two diaries – one for his religious work and the other for his work as an entertainer. Bill Latham helps him to schedule his religious work, often travelling with him to different churches on Sunday evenings, conducting question-and-answer sessions with Cliff in front of the congregation. Another frequent member of the entourage is David Winter, who wrote a biography of Cliff, *The Singer Not The Song*, and is editor of the religious periodical *Crusade*.

'My religious commitments are often scheduled two or three years in advance,' Cliff told me. 'With something like a crusade, where you may be appearing for several nights in a large hall, the details have to be carefully planned with advertising, posters, and so on so the organisers need to know well in advance that I will be available and that there is no question of my having to call it off at a later date . . . what happens is that my religious secretary phones the office and tells them which dates I've set aside, and then the office knows that I'm not available for TV or recording or anything like that on those dates . . . before I went on that South African crusade, the date had been in my diary for two and a half years . . . and the Japanese dates had been in my diary almost as long.'

Important though they are to him, those are the aspects of his religious work that are most known to the public and inevitably attract the widest publicity; but even on a week-to-week basis his diary is still arranged so that he is able to accept other much-less-publicised engagements and to take an active part in his own local church in Finchley.

Although Cliff went to Church regularly in childhood and says he was brought up in what he describes as 'a Church of England household', Cliff rebelled against all this during his teens and it was not until December 6th, 1966 – after he had already appeared on stage at the Earls Court Crusade with the American evangelist Dr Billy Graham – that he was confirmed by the Bishop of Willesden. And he has remained within the Church of England, even though two of his sisters have become Jehovah's Witnesses as has one of his closest friends within the music business Hank Marvin, lead guitarist with The Shadows since they became his backing group in 1958. Indeed, it was another Jehovah's Witness – the former Shadow Brian 'Licorice' Locking, who used to read his Bible every night on tour – who became one of the key influences in Cliff's life. It was while they were touring Australia together at a time when Cliff was feeling rather dispirited after the death of his father that he started discussing religion with Locking, who read him passages from the Bible, something that turned his own thinking back towards the faith of his childhood.

That Christmas of 1966, just after his confirmation, Cliff Richard was appearing as Buttons in the pantomime 'Cinderella' at the London Palladium. After the Christmas Eve performance, he drove back to his church in Finchley and took his first Christmas Communion. 'That was something that I shall always remember. It meant a great deal to me. The thing I really like about Christmas Eve services is that all my friends are there, and there is a tremendous family sort of feeling . . .

even if some of my friends cannot get to church every Sunday, they will all be there together on Christmas Eve, and I find it a lovely service for that reason.'

Nowadays, he seldom mentions the name of the church in interviews (and as he has asked me not to do so on occasions, I will respect that here) after having an uncomfortable feeling that there were some people starting to join the congregation more in the hope of seeing him than in a desire to worship. 'We seem to have got ourselves a floating congregation' was the way he put it.

It is this same basic congregation that he joins most Sundays with Bill Latham if he can; for some years now he has kept his Sundays free – and also his Tuesdays (when possible) so that he can spend the evenings playing badminton or tennis. It was through this church and his connections with his old school that he first became interested in youth organisations, and ultimately became President of the Members Council of the National Association of Youth Clubs.

First he became an active member of the Crusaders Union, helping a group of teacher friends to organise a weekly youth club for around seventy young teenagers in the area, organising games and outings as well as Bible readings. Most Easter holidays since 1965, he has spent a week or a fortnight with the club's members boating on the Norfolk Broads, where he now has his own boat, joining in like everyone else with the washing up, shopping, cooking, lighting of camp fires – and then in the evenings taking his guitar out of its case and playing a few songs. 'Every year when I open a new diary, Easter week is crossed off – and my manager (Peter Gormley) knows I'll be away camping then. He knows that I'll not be available for any other work that week,' said Cliff. Then on other days during the year he will help to organise outings for the members to places like London Airport and Whipsnade Zoo – and every Christmas he joins the members of the Crusader class carol-singing around the streets of Finchley.

'We've got it well organised now,' he says. 'Every year a few kids go round from door to door saying which nights we'll be singing, and then on the night we stand beneath the lamp posts, singing different carols, while other kids go from door to door with collection boxes, raising money for charity.'

Church on Sunday and the important occasions in the Christian calendar like Christmas and Easter are the highlights of his domestic life, and when he is not working or taking part in some other Church function Cliff tends to live just as quietly as any of his fans, curling up most evenings to watch TV, then hiking through the streets for 'midnight walkies' with his Labrador mongrel Kelly before reading his daily Bible passage, and going to bed.

He has always kept late hours, though he allots himself a precise eight hours-a-night in bed; the Bible-reading is part and parcel of his own commitment as a member of the Crusaders. 'The idea is that we should read the whole Bible in five years,' he says, adding that he makes no special point of returning to the same passages again and again. 'I read it all. The whole basis of a good life is there. I really want to do this. I believe in it. The Bible is stacked with information, and all our laws derive from it.' When I asked him to expand a little more on that, he replied: 'Well, take adultery and fornication. Nobody seems to care these days. But the Bible is against it and when you think about life and society you realise that it is against society's interests, too. I'm not being a prude or anything like that. It's just that I want to lead a moral life. After all, these are man's laws as well.'

In the simplicity of his religion, and the open way in which he espouses his beliefs, Cliff Richard lays himself wide open; within the music business – which is possibly the most tolerant community in the world – he is often joked about, and even ridiculed. But by making such a public avowal of his beliefs Cliff Richard *has* faced the world chin-first. He really should not be too surprised when occasionally a blow connects. And the world does tend to eye rather circumspectly those who face it thus. For my own part, I find Cliff Richard rather naive but, as I said before, totally sincere, highly literate, devoid of sham, possessed of courage – and no man's fool.

CHAPTER TWO

Cliff Richard was born in Lucknow, India, on October 14th, 1940. His real name is Harry Roger Webb. He takes his middle name from his late father, Roger Webb, who had also been born in India after Cliff's grandfather emigrated from London early this century. Cliff's mother, Mrs Dorothy Webb (she remarried after her husband's death and is now Mrs Dorothy Bodkin) was also born there.

'I've always understood that my grandfather was born in a house in Threadneedle Street in the City of London, but every time I pass through there all I can see is banks and insurance offices,' Cliff told me. 'Whenever I drive down Threadneedle Street, I always wonder where my grandfather's house is. The area has all been redeveloped now, and I've wondered what it was like in his day, and what sort of house the family lived in. There are no houses at all left in that area now.'

After India became an independent state in 1947, families like the Webbs soon realised that the country they had known all their lives could be their home no longer; anti-British feeling ran deep and there was also considerable tension and some rioting between the Hindus and the Mohammedans. However Cliff was not very aware of this because he was still only seven and a half years old when the family caught a boat back to England.

Cliff has told me that his memories of Lucknow and the other towns where his father worked like Cawnpore, Calcutta, Jaipur and Howrah are now 'very hazy'. He can remember the aunts and uncles, cousins, nephews and nieces that were part of his childhood as a second generation immigrant family, and the first school that he went to which was attached to their local church, St Thomas's, Lucknow, where even as a small child Cliff used to sing in the choir.

'I can remember little things like never going home to lunch from school, but always having my lunch brought to the school for me – often curries and stews in a plate kept warm with a napkin,' he related.

His father then worked as an area manager for Kellners, a large catering firm with branches in all those different Indian towns (Cliff describes them as 'the Fortes of India'). Every Christmas the firm used to organise a party for staff and their children, and that provides one of Cliff's most vivid early memories. 'I'd been longing for a tricycle, and my Dad told me that Father Christmas would be leaving his presents that year by the Christmas tree at the Kellners' party. We went to the party, and I ran over to the tree – I must have been around five years old at the time – and there was a tricycle with a card attached addressed to Harry Webb. I ran all round the room shouting, "Is there anyone else here called Harry Webb?" because I just couldn't belief that tricycle could be mine. That was the biggest Christmas excitement that I can ever remember having as a child, because I had been really building up towards getting that tricycle.'

In those days, the Webb family had a large house with servants – and from what he has told me Cliff's life seems to have been a sheltered one. Until they had to leave for England, there were no hard times to live through – and even then his father seems to have been protective towards Cliff and his sisters Donella, Jacqueline and Joan. Cliff even continued believing in Father Christmas long past the age when most children discover his true identity. 'I must have been eleven or twelve years old before I stopped believing in Father Christmas,' Cliff told me. 'I'd had my doubts, as all children do, and then some time before Christmas I can remember going up to my Dad and saying, "There isn't really a Father Christmas, is there?" and he knew I'd rumbled it, and told me, "No." From then on that particular magic had gone. When you are very young, the whole magic of Christmas is that Father Christmas has come along with a present specially for you. It never occurs to you that someone must have paid for it, and you never stop to think what a wonderful coincidence it is that he always seems to know just what you want. The marvellous thing is that this kind man has brought you just what you want – and it's free.'

'While we were out in India, my father was very well off. He had a good job out there, and was earning good money. At Christmas, there was always a big bag full of toys. But when we came back to England, it was very different; he was quite hard up, and there was all the difference between a big bag of presents one Christmas – and a small sock the next which a child finds very hard to understand. That first Christmas when I no longer believed, I still woke up several times in the night, wondering if they would still put something there at the end of the bed after all. I can remember lying in bed, and poking my feet through the blanket – but each time I woke up there was nothing there. That was quite sad, I suppose, looking back . . . there's no excitement quite the same as being a child at Christmas. I can remember another year when I woke up, poked my feet down the bed – and there was a train set. There's nothing that can compare with a thrill like that.'

Another very vivid memory that Cliff retains of India is kite-flying because to children living there kites were one of the most popular of all toys – and not just for children. 'I used to sit for hours on the roof of our house watching my Dad flying kites, and it was fascinating,' said Cliff, describing the many-coloured kites with their different shapes, brightly painted faces and fluttering tails. 'In India kite-flying was always taken very seriously, and the aim was to "tangle" with other people flying their kites so that theirs are dashed to the ground. You take your cotton kite string and rub in a mixture of white of egg and finely powdered ground glass, so that by the time it's rubbed in the string has a sharp cutting edge.

'Then you fly the kites, which are all totally mobile, and try to fly your kite across the path of your opponent's so that you can cut his string by a quick jerk on your own. The trick is to play with the strings so that you "tangle" his kite as well as cutting the string – and then you can claim his kite as your prize . . . but with strings as sharp as that, you have to be careful not to cut yourself because they're like razors and you just have to wear leather gloves.'

Although fighting broke out in the streets around the time of Indian Independence, and Cliff can remember hearing the sound of guns being fired, he says he never saw any violence. 'For a time, the only place that I was allowed to play was in the back yard – but they never tried to attack our house because a rumour had gone round the area (we were then living in Lucknow again) that my Dad had an elephant gun. The rumour was quite true; he had had one – but by then he had sold it. Nevertheless, the rumour probably saved us because no-one came near the house. Next door to us was a derelict sewing machine factory and I can remember at one time when the fighting became really bad that there was a Mohammedan refugee hiding in there. For two days we threw bread and other food over the wall for him, and then after that we smuggled him into the house, and hid him there until it was safe for him to go out again.'

Cliff never saw his father shoot an elephant, but he does remember him going off tiger-hunting – though he can never remember him bringing a tiger back. 'I'm sure if he had shot one, I'd have known about it – there'd have been a tiger skin rug or a head on the wall. At the very least, there'd have been talk about it in the family,' he says. He can also remember travelling on a train that sounds very like a scene from a film; largely wooden carriages with people crammed in the compartments. 'That was between Lucknow and Buxa when I went to stay with my grandparents, and I can remember that because I had an uncle who was a year younger than I was – that was because my mother's mother had married a second time and had a second family.

'The most dangerous thing I can remember doing out there is bee-hunting, which we used to think was great fun – my mother tells me that I was pretty vicious with animals when I was a very young child. We used to go chasing bees with our badminton rackets, killing them by the hundred – which was a very dangerous thing to do. I'm horrified now that I ever did it because if the bees had swarmed, they could have killed us – and my sister did get stung once in the ear. For years after that every time she heard a bee buzzing, she would instinctively cover her ears with her hands.'

His father was undoubtedly a very strong influence on Cliff both then and later on in his professional career. He was a man used to commanding employees, demanding discipline in his home, urging his children to live by Christian principles including Bible reading every night in the family home. Although later in his mid teens Cliff rebelled against this and restrictions like having to be in by 10 pm at night, it can hardly have been a normal home background for they were after all an immigrant family in a country where the native population was flexing its muscles as India gained independence from the British. But Cliff says he was largely unaware of that, though he did tell his friend David Winter (who wrote the book *New Singer, New Song*) that he remembered a crowd of Indians jostling them when he was out shopping with his mother, and one of them shouting, 'Why don't you go home to your own country, white woman?'

Being just a child, Cliff's own interests were much more fundamental; playing ball games in the yard outside their home, watching the monkeys with their bright red bottoms jumping from branch to branch – 'we used to pull faces at them, and they'd chase us' – and the normal mischief of childhood.

'When I was a little kid, I'd eat anything I could get my hands on,' he told me. 'My mother's told me that my Dad would often dive across the floor just in time to stop me popping a lizard in my mouth, because there were lizards all round the house out there . . . I'd put anything in my mouth, grass, flowers, twigs, anything I could lay my fingers on. I can remember hearing my Dad say once that if you dropped a cat, he would always land on his feet so I got our cat and took him upstairs and then dropped him through the bedroom window. My Dad was right, of course. The cat did land on his feet – and ran away as fast as his legs could carry him.

'Another thing I can remember, which shows that my mother must be right when she says that I was pretty vicious towards animals as a child (she says I was always testing them to see how far they'd go), was that we used to have a green parrot that we kept in a cage. He used to whistle away in his cage and one day apparently I put a cloth toy parrot in his cage for him to play with – though I didn't mean to hurt him. Anyway, our parrot kept attacking this cloth parrot and was going quite frantic, and by the time my Dad came home, the real parrot was dead – he had pecked the cloth parrot to tiny pieces and had collapsed with the exhaustion and excitement of it all.'

All this ended when Mr and Mrs Webb decided that for all the comfort of their home and the apparent security that his job with Kellners gave them, the future for British families in India was just too uncertain; the violence was growing and coming closer and closer to their own doorstep, and they were beginning to fear for their own safety and that of their children.

The Webbs were torn between two destinations. Many immigrant families were leaving India at that time, and some of their friends were planning to move on to Australia; but the Webbs decided against that, and spent all their savings buying boat tickets back to Britain, returning to the home country that neither of them had ever seen.

For them, it must have been a traumatic experience. Money was very short, and the family arrived in England with only £5 in cash, travelling to Carshalton, where they lived for nearly eighteen months, with Mr Webb out of work for much of the time, and dependant on help from relatives while he struggled to find a job at a time when unemployment was high.

But for Cliff it was all an adventure – as it would have been for any child to travel across the oceans by boat, an old troop ship packed with bunks. By day, he could swim in the canvas swimming pools on deck; by night there were film shows – and then when the family arrived in England there was all the excitement of meeting relatives he had heard of and never seen. One thing that Cliff says he remembers clearly was the flowers on Carshalton Station – and the greenery of the fields which was something he had never seen before.

They had all arrived in England in September, 1948, and Cliff was enrolled at the Stanley Park Road Primary School in Carshalton, where his skin was so dark-tanned after all his years in India that the other children would shout out 'nigger' and 'where's your head-dress' thinking that India was the home of cowboys and Indians! When I have asked Cliff about his childhood, he has never said very much about Carshalton, which does not seem to have been a particularly happy period in his life – though he did once tell me that it was there that he first had a girlfriend. 'Her name was Elizabeth Sayers, and she was about the same age as me. She had long hair in a pony tail, and I used to walk her home – and that's about all I can remember about her now,' he says.

Eventually his father did find a job – after the family had moved right across the other side of London to live with Mr Webb's sister in Waltham Cross, all cramped together in one room while they awaited their turn for a council house. The job that Mr Webb found was working in the Ferguson's radio factory at Enfield, while Mrs Webb also found a job in another factory at Broxbourne so that the family would have two pay packets coming into the house as they re-established themselves. While they were out at work, Cliff was at his new school – the Kings Road Primary School in Waltham Cross, where he won a prize for his work, although he still failed to pass his 11-plus examinations, much to his parents' anxiety since they had been anxious that he should go on to the local grammar school.

Eventually, they decided that Cliff should go to the Cheshunt Secondary Modern School, having been offered a small, red-brick, three-bedroomed council house on the local council estate – an offer which came when a housing officer from the local council was horrified to learn that they were all living together in that one small room. Although delighted to have a home of their own at last after living with relatives for two years, the Webbs still had no furniture of their own; all theirs had been left behind in India. 'My father bought packing cases for a shilling each and made two armchairs. My mother cried a lot,' Cliff was to recall many years later in an interview with *The Daily Telegraph* colour supplement.

The family had had some hard knocks, and though Cliff is not a person to dwell overmuch on such aspects of his life, there must have been a feeling of failure in the family as they struggled to start anew. This may be why Cheshunt Secondary Modern School was to prove so important to him. There were teachers there who were genuinely dedicated, particularly his English teacher Mrs Norris, and he developed friendships that have continued to this day; friendships that run extraordinarily deep so that he still goes back to the school regularly, supports its functions, and now shares a home with one of the teachers he met through the school, Bill Latham.

But then he was still very much a growing boy, and from one story he told me probably a very sensitive one. One day he said he was standing in the back garden holding an air gun, shooting tin cans off the back fence with one of his friends. 'This boy saw a starling sitting on the fence, and said "Try and shoot that". I just turned, and shot the rifle from the hip – and it dropped down dead. Great waves of conscience swept over me, and I was suddenly very ashamed at the realisation that I had actually killed a living creature. It was something that I had never felt when I was younger out in India, and it was then that I realised how wrong it was to hurt birds and animals. When you are very young your feelings are not so finely developed, and I think all little boys are rather callous at times, but after shooting that starling I know that I would be pretty hopeless if it ever came to being a soldier. I could never bring myself to shoot another human being. I know that emotionally it is something that I just couldn't do.'

The friendships that Cliff developed at school, with fellow pupils as well as teachers, run very deep; far more so than with most people. Two of them were John and Michael Kingdom, who lived next door to the Webb family in those days, and whose mother, Mrs Gwen Kingdom, told me: 'Cliff was very happy at school, and he has kept on coming back since he left. He was always very different to the other boys living around here at that time. He was a very well-mannered and nicely-spoken boy – his mother always used to insist on that. When my family were all taken ill, the other lads in the neighbourhood used to run errands and do the shopping for us, but they always expected sixpence for doing it – but not Cliff, though I still used to offer it to him. One day, he did accept the sixpence when I offered it to him – and his mother made him bring it straight back to me. "Mummy says it's a poor show if I have to be paid every time I go down to the shops," he told me.

'Like most children in the neighbourhood, Cliff was always playing cowboys and Indians with my lads and the other boys they played with. When they started off, they had rubber stickers on the end of their arrows – but some of the lads started getting adventurous, strapping iron nails on the end of their arrows to fire at one another. We parents didn't know anything about this until one day we heard a terrible scream coming from the park across the road. I ran across and there was Cliff rolling about on the ground clutching his foot. One of those arrows had gone straight through his foot. There were no more bows and arrows after that. His mother made sure of that.'

Mrs Kingdom revealed that it was when Cliff was just coming into his teens that he first became interested in religion (he has himself since told me that in his later teens he rebelled against it): 'His mother did not like Cliff making too much noise on Sundays, and I remember one week Cliff was playing football on the village green when his mother called him inside. I asked her later whether she had done that because they all went to Church together on Sundays, and she told me that it wasn't that at all. It was because she believed that all families should be together on a Sunday evening, reading the Bible. She could be very firm with him – but I noticed that she relented a little bit when Cliff started getting interested in music. When he was playing in different groups, the boys used to go round to their place on Sunday afternoons to practise. But funnily enough Cliff never acted like a pop singer at all. Even when his group started getting bookings at the local youth clubs and dance halls, you would always see him in a suit – a blue one. And I don't know why, but he always wore brown leather gloves – even in summer.

'We had heard all about him going in for talent shows and going away to Butlins' holiday camp, and then one day it happened – he got his big break, a booking on "Oh Boy!", which was the television show that all the youngsters watched in those days. Everyone around here stayed in that evening, glued to their TV sets, and we all felt so proud because we knew him – and he was marvellous. That night I met him at the bus stop after he had come back from London on the train, and told him he looked hungry – and he admitted that he had been so nervous that day that he just couldn't eat. All he had had all day was a biscuit.'

Mrs Kingdom is convinced that if it had not been for his mother, the Cliff Richard success story might never have happened. 'She always was a wonderful woman, and very determined, and I often think that he wouldn't have got where he is today if it hadn't been for her,' she told me. 'He was always devoted to his parents, and was very upset when his father died – and I wasn't really surprised when I read years later that he had thought of becoming a teacher. It all seemed to fit, somehow.'

By the time of that first appearance on the Jack Good produced ABC TV series 'Oh Boy!' Cliff had already been playing with different groups for three years – and was now nearly eighteen years old. He had entered talent contests, played at local dances, tried his luck in the coffee bars that were the big attraction for the skiffle groups of the day. One of those he played at was the 2Is coffee bar in Old Compton Street, Soho, where it just so happened that one night a very young Marc Bolan – who was then working on his mother's stall in the nearby Berwick Street Market – was standing near the doorway. He saw Cliff being shown to the door, and heard him being told: 'Forget it, Harry – you'll never make it!'

This was a time when teenagers all over Britain were trying to play skiffle like Lonnie Donegan, who had caught their imagination with the suggestion that they, too, could sound like that with the help of a washboard, a tea-chest bass and maybe a guitar – but Cliff was much more interested in the American rock 'n' roll stars like Bill Haley and the Comets, Elvis Presley, Little Richard, Gene Vincent and Carl Perkins. While still at Cheshunt Secondary Modern School and a prefect, he played truant one day to get tickets for a Haley concert at Edmonton – and had a shock next morning when the Headmaster took back his prefect's badge. His English teacher, Mrs Norris, told him: 'In ten years' time, I'll bet you won't even remember the name of Bill Haley.' Cliff, by now very keen on pop music, replied to her: 'I'll bet you I will, miss – I'll bet you a box of chocolates that I will!' Ten years later Mrs Norris, who remains to this day one of Cliff's closest personal friends, paid up and gave him that box of chocolates.

While he was still at Cheshunt Secondary Modern School, she often teased him about wanting to be a rock 'n' roll singer – but it was nevertheless she who first suggested that he should join a group (one within the school called The Quintones which often used to perform at school concerts); it was she who encouraged him to appear in a school dramatic society production based on Kenneth Grahame's *Wind In The Willows* (in which he sang two numbers as Ratty), and it is no doubt significant that the only subject in which he was eventually successful in his General Certificate of Education examinations was the one that she taught, English. Had he been more successful in those examinations Cliff thinks that he might well have become a bank clerk or possibly even then a teacher; as it was with just that one result on his GCE certificate his father found him a job at the Ferguson's factory as a credit control clerk in their offices.

One evening Cliff was at home when a boy who lived in the neighbourhood, Terry Smart, called and asked whether he would like to join a local group, The Dick Teague Skiffle Group, in which he was the drummer – and because they were already friends, when Cliff said he could not play an instrument Terry gave him a guitar. Over the next few weeks Cliff spent every waking moment learning to play that guitar, mastering his first chords and it was to prove the beginning of his group career.

After a few months with the Dick Teague group he and Terry Smart formed their own group, The Drifters – not Harry Webb and the Drifters or Cliff Richard and the Drifters, but just The Drifters – and it was then that they started making their first appearances at the 21s coffee bar, where they met another keen young musician Ian Samwell, who was to later write Cliff's first hit single 'Move It' and who was also a member of The Drifters. He just walked up to them one night in the 21s, wearing his Royal Air Force uniform, asked if he could join them, and explained that in just a few days he was due to finish his National Service and would like to join a group.

That was early in 1958, and years later in the 1964 *New Musical Express* annual Ian Samwell recalled: 'He (Cliff) was very Elvis Presley-ish . . . Terry Smart stuck with us for ages. He eventually left the group after I did. He's now in the Merchant Navy. But nobody really replaced Norman (their rhythm guitarist Norman Mitcham) for a while. A man came into the 21s and booked us into a hall near Nottingham. But he said he wouldn't book us as The Drifters. We had to have a name. We found Cliff Richard: the surname was a dedication to Little Richard . . . about this time George Ganjou saw an advert we put out, came and heard us and booked us for a Saturday morning teenage show in a theatre in Shepherds Bush. Then he came and told us to make a demonstration disc. We did "Lawdy Miss Clawdy", which was the big Elvis Presley number at that time, and "Great Balls of Fire", which was a Jerry Lee Lewis hit. You can see the kind of music we played then – out-and-out rock.'

That recording cost just six pounds to produce, and Ganjou sent it off to Norrie Paramor, Recording Manager for the

Columbia label at EMI, who invited them to his office. There they set up their equipment, played the numbers again – and were told that he would record them after returning from a holiday that he was just about to start. 'That was one of the longest fortnights of my life,' Cliff has said many times since. He was still working at the Ferguson's radio factory, and yet he could not help wondering while he waited for Paramor to come back from his two weeks' holiday whether this might not be the start of something. After all, by then Tommy Steele had already had his first hit records and all over the country there were teenagers thinking and dreaming that their chance might come next. Up in Liverpool John Lennon and Paul McCartney were already thinking their chance might come, and had been playing together for two years.

Once Paramor had shown interest and offered Cliff a recording contract, events moved very quickly for him. A song publisher Franklin Boyd brought Paramor a song that he thought was suitable for Cliff, "Schoolboy Crush", which he duly recorded – and then Ian Samwell came up with another song that was chosen as the B-side, 'Move It'. (When the record was released it was 'Move It' that became the hit). George Ganjou, who was by then Cliff's agent, obtained a four-week booking for him and his group at the Butlins' holiday camp at Clacton-on-Sea – and on the strength of that Cliff gave up his job at the Ferguson factory in August, 1958 (the last words he heard from his boss were: 'You were never cut out to be a clerk, anyway!').

The reason why 'Move It' became the hit was that Franklin Boyd took the single down to Jack Good, who was then the most influential figure in the music business, producing the programme 'Oh Boy!' (he had also produced '6.5 Special') which was the shop window for all the new songs of the day – and when Good heard the two songs he said quite bluntly that 'Move It' was the better side. Good invited Cliff to appear on the show, making his TV debut – and becoming a regular in the series.

Cliff made that television debut on 'Oh Boy!' on September 13th, 1958. Two weeks later he entered the *New Musical Express* chart for the first time at No 28. The pace quickened – he was booked to support the Kalin Twins, an American duo whose single 'When' had recently been a No 1 hit in Britain (it was the one and only hit they ever had here) and who had been brought over for a British concert tour. That opened at the Victoria Hall, Hanley, on October 5th – and that same month Cliff made his radio debut on the BBC Light Programme's 'Saturday Club'. The following month, November, he made his variety debut at the old Metropolitan theatre in Edgware Road, London.

When that tour with the Kalin Twins opened, Cliff's group was still called The Drifters – and its members then were Ian Samwell on bass guitar, Terry Smart on drums, and two newcomers from Newcastle, Hank Marvin and Bruce Welch, who had both been playing down at the 21s in Soho. In that article in the *New Musical Express* annual, Samwell said: 'Originally, we wanted to get Tony Sheridan who has since become a very big name in Germany on the Hamburg beat scene. But Tony wasn't there that night. Hank and Bruce were, however. For Cliff it was a big step to have two newcomers, but neither Hank nor Bruce wanted the job without the other, so both came. Norman (Mitcham) left and I moved over to bass guitar with Terry still on drums. By now the nucleus of the group had formed. Cliff was able to stop playing guitar. Jet Harris was on the tour with us, playing for the Most Brothers. He played bass guitar and was so good that we all realised he had to join the group. So I left . . . Tony Meehan joined a couple of months after Jet (replacing Terry Smart on drums). He and Jet had played together with the Vipers Skiffle Group. For a time I was manager of the newly named Shadows. It lasted about nine months, although there wasn't much I could do because they were closely tied up with Cliff.'

Thus, by early 1959, it was Cliff Richard and The Shadows – with a line-up that was to remain constant for the next three years. To this day Marvin and Welch are still closely associated with him, as is Meehan, though in a much less conspicuous way. But Jet Harris was to prove one of the saddest casualties of British rock 'n' roll.

CHAPTER THREE

Until The Beatles suddenly burst through early in 1963 with a sound and a style that revolutionised the music business both in this country and throughout the world, Cliff Richard and The Shadows were the most successful group that Britain had ever produced. They won nearly every available award, starred in summer shows and pantomimes, made highly successful films, toured Scandinavia, South Africa, the United States and Australia and had a run of hit records that had until then never been equalled. Between August, 1958, when 'Move It' brought him his first success, and March, 1963, when The Beatles topped the charts for the first time, Cliff Richard had issued twenty singles. Of those, six went to No 1 in the music paper charts, another eight reached No 2 – and all twenty were Top Ten entries. There had never been another success story like it.

Both on that first single and again with the second 'High Class Baby'/'My Feet Hit The Ground', which was released in November, 1958, Cliff recorded largely with session musicians – but by January, 1959, the line-up of The Shadows had been settled. They made their first appearance together that month at the Free Trade Hall in Manchester, and thereafter the group played with him permanently both on stage and in recording sessions until The Shadows themselves disbanded in mid-December, 1968.

Over the years there were frequent changes in The Shadows' line-up, but Hank Marvin and Bruce Welch remained – and even after The Shadows broke up they continued to work closely with Cliff, sometimes joining him to record, appearing on TV shows together, latterly with their own trio Marvin, Welch and Farrar (the third member is the Australian John Farrar), and more recently still Marvin and Welch re-formed The Shadows and were asked to represent Britain in the 1975 Eurovision Song Contest (see Chapter Four which tells the Shadows' role in the Cliff Richard story and their own success quite independently from him).

Cliff himself became the ultimate seemingly stereo-styled late-Fifties-early-Sixties pop star – his smile was as constant as the morning sunrise; he loved his parents and his sisters; bought the family a succession of houses; seldom said a word out of place; never smoked; rarely drank anything other than an occasional glass of wine; told the world that his favourite food and drink were Indian curry and rice plus Tizer (with ice cream); always had his hair short and well-groomed, and as time went by put on weight and became rather chubby (he soon stopped that after hearing Minnie Caldwell say on 'Coronation Street' that she did like 'that chubby Cliff Richard').

It was an image that was easy to mock, and when The Beatles and the other rough-around-the-edges rock groups emerged in the 1963 Mersey Beat boom mock they did. John Lennon in particular was frequently caustic about Cliff Richard's style and his music – but the reality was that there was nothing false about his image at all.

He really was rather conventional in outlook, very well-mannered, did look after his family carefully (which is not so surprising after all they had been through together), was fastidious about his personal appearance – that wasn't a well-groomed puppet that you may remember seeing on TV years ago singing 'Living Doll' and all his teenage love songs. It was the real Cliff Richard. And though many of the more hard-bitten rock groups who had kept going on pills and booze, who had whored through most cities in Europe, who had scraped for money and fought with their fists when times were hard have found it hard to believe Cliff Richard really was no phoney. He was just being himself.

Perhaps the key figure in his life in those very early days of his career was his father, who gave up his job at the Ferguson factory – and quickly showed a detailed grasp of the business aspects of Cliff's career, scrutinised his contracts, and was very firm with his successive managers and agents. In the very beginning when Cliff was part of The Drifters their gigs had been arranged for around five pounds a night by a north London agent Johnny Foster; later it was George Ganjou who handled their bookings while at the same time – at the suggestion of Norrie Paramor – the song publisher Franklin Boyd became Cliff's manager, though that was an arrangement that did not last very long. In law, Cliff was still a minor and under the age of consent (which was then twenty-one) – and when his father found that Cliff had been over-working he stepped in and cancelled the agreement with Boyd. This was highly controversial at the time, but Cliff explained why in the book *It's Great To Be Young* (published in 1960 by Souvenir Press): 'We were all so excited about what was happening that we didn't know that I wasn't getting the necessary expert advice. But there came a certain time during the run of "Oh Boy!" when I was not only rehearsing for that show but I was doing a week's variety at the Finsbury Park Empire, also going down to the film studios making "Serious Charge"; I even had a Jack Jackson TV appearance as well; that's right, all in the same week! Now I can tell you that any one of those jobs is quite enough for one week's work . . . by the end of the week not only had I just about lost my voice but, on the Saturday night, after the last show at the Finsbury Park Empire, I crawled home and collapsed into bed. I didn't just go to sleep that night, I died. And I didn't wake up to the alarm when it went off the following morning . . . I came to with Mum shaking me by the shoulder saying I simply had to get up or I'd be late. I just broke down. "Mum, I can't stand this life any more. If it's going to be like this I'd sooner go back and get my old job at the factory." And I meant it . . . and Dad did what any father would do when he wrote to Franklin and told him that he didn't want him to manage me any more.'

After Franklin Boyd, the former comedian and bandleader Tito Burns became Cliff's manager – and though that relationship was also fairly short-lived Burns went on to become one of Britain's most successful agents and one of the leading executives in the early days of London Weekend Television. In 1960, the Australian Peter Gormley who had brought Frank Ifield to England became Cliff's personal manager – and that same year Leslie Grade, head of the Grade Organisation, became Cliff's personal agent. These two relationships were to prove lasting; Grade and Gormley are still handling Cliff's affairs today, with no contracts to bind them. It has been a relationship based wholly on trust throughout. I can remember some years ago Cliff telling me that during his first year with Gormley the Australian claimed no commission because he thought it would be wrong to do so on commitments that had been negotiated before his appointment.

And so, at a time when many of the other groups that were to emerge to challenge him were either still at school or being fleeced by provincial agents or swindled by smalltime ballroom promoters, there was Cliff Richard – the epitome of respectability both in his private life and in his personal and business relationships. 'Cliff is the perfect star', recording manager Norrie Paramor was to tell the *New Musical Express*. 'He is so easy to work with, so polite, so even tempered. He knows what he wants and he gets it without any tantrums.' And I must say that in all the years that I have interviewed Cliff Richard he has always been extremely courteous, friendly, anxious to help in every way and totally professional in each detail. To this day he is remarkably modest and lacking in pretension – and yet at the same time there is a curious emptiness about any discussion one has with him. Quite often I have finished long interviews with other artistes with the feeling that I have learned something new or thought about life or music in a different way – and not infrequently felt that I have been exchanging ideas and conversation with people of quite exceptional talent. Paul McCartney, Marc Bolan, David Bowie, David Essex, Denny Laine, Pete Townshend, Roger Daltrey, Charlie Watts, Jon Anderson, Steve Howe, Robert Plant, Rick Wakeman, John Entwistle, Labi Siffre – it's by no means a definitive list: I could name at least fifty more performers and musicians to whom one could talk and at once be aware by their choice of words and the way the conversation develops that these were people of rare quality who could have risen to the top of several other branches of the Arts. Never once have I had that feeling after talking to Cliff Richard, and while I am perfectly prepared to admit that it is quite possible that he *may* possess hidden depths that are so well-shielded that my questions have never penetrated I suspect that the real explanation is that Cliff Richard is just what he seems.

And that provokes the question how has he managed to last so long? How is it that Cliff Richard is the great survivor – the one person who goes on collecting awards, getting hit records (he has now had over sixty, which is more than The Beatles or the Rolling Stones or any other performer with the exception of Elvis Presley), who stage shows are always highly successful?

The answer is in my view quite extraordinarily simple: he has never stopped working, seldom strayed from the area of music that he has made his own, always kept supplying *his* audience with the type of material that they have shown they like, always avoided the peril of self-indulgence (which destroys more careers in music than anything else), seldom had anything even approaching bad publicity, never been involved in any scandals, and in the process has developed a lifestyle that is genuinely simple, honestly Christian and almost flawless.

Perhaps the most extraordinary feature of his whole story is that his career more than any other artiste demonstrates just what can be achieved by the blend of a totally professional outlook on the part of the performer accompanied by skilled management. Once an artiste reaches a certain level of success, the important thing is that he and those around him know what *not* to do – and what his audience expects of him.

In this respect, Cliff Richard's career is a model (as you can see from the chronological sequence of events described in the appendix): his records have always maintained a high level of quality and have been just what his audience likes; the films have been aimed at just the same audience; his regular concert tours, summer shows (in the early days), pantomimes and TV appearances have kept him constantly available for that audience (but not so constantly that they have ever been able to get bored), and one can but admire the apparent inevitability of it all.

I once began an interview with Cliff Richard by asking him what had happened to him since the last time we had spoken. Most artistes would have answered with a series of anecdotes, telling me where they had travelled, what they had written, whom they had met, but Cliff just said: 'Nothing, nothing ever happens to me . . . life just goes on and on.' It seemed such an extraordinary thing for a major artiste to say that I probed as deeply as I could – and found that he was being quite truthful. Nothing had happened to him that was in any way out of the ordinary: he had been to Church as usual every Sunday, played badminton most Tuesday evenings, recorded a few more songs, made some personal appearances on TV and in concert, taken his dog for a walk every night, kept up his daily

Bible readings, seen a few cinema films, had his usual holidays at his other home in Portugal and boating on the Norfolk Broads, and that was about it. By most people's standards, it was a full and varied life – but it had changed little from the year before.

Though it is easy to play down his achievements and to over-stress the routine, it would still be wrong to do so – for the very fact that he has worked so hard for nearly twenty years, has maintained his track record and the loyalty of his fans and that he has in so doing out-stripped the other singers and groups who started when he did is in itself quite remarkable. (Tommy Steele and Adam Faith are the two other stars of his generation who have stayed right there at the top, but each in a different way.) Cliff Richard's changes in presentation over that time have been few.

In the beginning, back in 1958, his style appeared to be closely modelled on Elvis Presley with faint Teddy Boy undertones. Cliff arrived complete with curling lip, long sideburns, a quiff of greasy hair and tight trousers; his stage-act was ever-so-slightly suggestive and twitching hips and sultry glances across the footlights as he stood at the microphone (the Press even called him 'crude', 'indecent' and 'vulgar' in those days); his jackets were occasionally pink with black trousers, black shirts and pink ties. This is what I remember him wearing the first time I saw Cliff Richard and The Shadows on stage in 1959 shortly after the success of 'Living Doll', which was his first No 1 hit. By the beginning of the following year, when he and The Shadows made their first and only US concert tour, the sideburns had been trimmed and the Teddy Boy undertones had gone – Cliff was now dressed all in white and The Shadows all in black. Within a few months, the image had changed again with Cliff now crossing the teenage barriers, singing ballads, appealing to parents as well as their daughters – and dressed in almost conventional dark suits, white shirts and discreet ties.

The changes in style happened in sequence just like the changes in his management and agency representation; if any mistakes were made they were probably that Cliff Richard tried to do too much too soon – certainly that US tour came very early in his career, before he had in any way established himself in the States. In retrospect, it would probably have been better for him to have waited a while before going over there; then there would have been that much more mystery surrounding him as an overseas artist before the tour. But it is easy to be critical; back in those days it was felt to be a major break-through for a British artist to be invited to tour the States.

That tour of America began in January, 1960, just as Cliff Richard was having his sixth hit single in Britain (the dates are given in sequence in the appendix). He had followed the success of 'Move It' with two more singles 'High Class Baby' and 'Never Mind'/'Mean Streak' before getting his first two Number 1 hits with 'Living Doll' (which brought him his first Gold Disc for sales of over 1,000,000) and 'Travelling Light'. Then he had turned to ballads with that sixth single 'A Voice In The Wilderness', which had reached Number 2 in the music paper charts.

In just eighteen months, he and The Shadows (who had had to change their name from The Drifters to avoid confusion with the American vocal group) appeared on nearly every major TV show, and won numerous awards such as the *New Musical Express* Singer of the Year Award for 1959, the *Melody Maker* Record of the Year and Singer of the Year Awards after 'Living Doll', the Best Singer Award for 1959 and 1960 from the ATV programme 'Cool for Cats', and an Ivor Novello Award for 'Living Doll'.

But in the process his image had changed far too suddenly. Whereas a year earlier, in December 1958 when he was appearing regularly on Jack Good's 'Oh Boy!' TV series the *New Musical Express* had felt fit to describe his act as 'the most crude exhibitionism ever seen on British TV', as being 'hardly the kind of performance any parent could wish their children to witness' and had added the suggestion that 'if we are expected to believe that Cliff Richard was acting "naturally" then consideration for medical treatment before it's too late may be advisable', now he was suddenly wholesome. Not quite the Vicar of Pop, maybe – but certainly every mother's ideal son (or son-in-law).

In a business where image and style are so important, transitions can be made; as artistes mature and develop they can change their appearance and public personality – as The Beatles did so very successfully when they threw off the 'mop top' image, and as Gilbert O'Sullivan did when he abandoned his Chaplinesque style of presentation. But it is my view that in Cliff Richard's case, the transition did not seem to happen naturally. He switched from rock 'n' roll – from being the teenage rebel to the polished balladeer – before he had consolidated his position as a rock 'n' roll singer. This may have been intentional; it was a widely held view in those days that rock 'n' roll music would prove to be a very short-lived fad. Tommy Steele had successfully started to move on, and now Cliff Richard had moved away from what I believe to be quite genuine roots – and had even made his first film appearances in 'Serious Charge' and in 'Espresso Bongo', films that were good in their day and an ideal showcase for a pop star anxious to become an all-round entertainer, but which nevertheless featured Cliff in roles that did not bring forward his own personality and which could have been played with equal or better effect by any one of a generation of young actors just leaving drama school. And that was not all – Cliff Richard and The Shadows even appeared in pantomime at the Stockton Globe in 'Babes In The Wood', no less!

This was certainly traditional 'show biz' – but to the generation of young musicians by now starting to play in youth clubs and ballrooms throughout the Midlands, Tyneside and Merseyside, who had been fired by rock 'n' roll, who lived it every day, and who wanted to make hit records themselves so that they could be up there with Gene Vincent, Little Richard and Jerry Lee Lewis, all this was an anathema.

And before the transition had even been fully accomplished, Cliff Richard and The Shadows flew off to the States to tour with Frankie Avalon, Bobby Rydell, Johnny and the Hurricanes and Clyde McPhatter, travelling as much as 700 or 800 miles a day by Greyhound coach to get to each gig. The tour itinerary shows that this could have been their major breakthrough – they opened in Montreal at the Forum on January 22nd, and then played in Pennsylvania, Toronto, Ontario, Indianapolis, Ohio, Michigan, Kentucky, Pittsburgh, New Jersey, Virginia, North Carolina, Texas, Oklahoma City, Kansas, Omaha, St Louis, Missouri and ending in Milwaukee on the 27th.

It was an impressive schedule, interrupted by just a few days when Cliff flew back to Britain on a round-trip to appear on 'Sunday Night At The London Palladium' and at the *New Musical Express* annual Poll Winners Concert at Wembley. Later he spent a week in New York, being interviewed for American magazines – and making a guest appearance on Pat Boone's TV show. Many of the tour's venues are still important ones for today's top rock groups. And while it is true that 'Living Doll' had been a minor hit for him in the States, it is nevertheless my view that Cliff Richard and The Shadows should have waited and paced themselves until they had had at least two or three hit singles in the US before undergoing a concert tour like that.

But it was still a great adventure for them to be able to visit American towns in Texas and the Far West that had until then been places they had only heard of through the movies. They visited the tourist area outside Oklahoma City where there is a reconstructed cowboy prairie township, complete with wooden sidewalks, saloons with swinging doors, mirrors behind the bar and bullet-holes in the furniture; they also went to the area where the famous Battle of the Alamo was fought, and in a museum saw Davy Crockett's vest and Jim Bowie's famous knife; they drove through the fields of Kentucky famous for their racehorse studs, and Cliff and his father met Elvis Presley's father and were taken back to see Presley's home. In the *Daily Telegraph* interview, Cliff said of that occasion: 'His picture (Presley's) was woven on the carpet as you came in: it was a fantastic place. When I got home a fan wove a picture of me into a carpet. I gave it to my mother. She keeps it at the end of her bed.' In that same interview, he said the opening night of that tour had been 'the greatest thrill I ever had. We and Clyde McPhatter stopped the show.'

Although he had turned to ballads more and more on that tour, and in the months preceding it when he released 'A Voice In The Wilderness' and starred in that Stockton pantomime, the group's music was still more rock 'n' roll-influenced; but in the months and years that followed rock seemed a lesser influence as they became more and more an act with family appeal – and by the time The Beatles and the other Liverpool, Birmingham and Manchester groups had taken rock music back to the States in 1964 Cliff Richard and The Shadows had moved well away from that kind of music.

In some ways I have always felt that his is a sad story; Cliff Richard was the first major British rock 'n' roll star – but he moved on too soon. Whether this was what he wanted to do, we shall never know; looking back now one is only being wise after the event. But the fact remains that when rock 'n' roll music was re-born again with The Beatles, Cliff Richard had been left behind with the ballads. In the process he had become a star with a very different following – he now had an audience that had apparently never been very rock 'n' roll conscious, that was probably of a much wider age range, that really did want to see groups that were smartly dressed, short-haired and knew how to dance; a fan following that has stayed with him ever since.

He was no longer a rock 'n' roll star – but an all round entertainer equally at home on 'Sunday Night At The London Palladium', on 'The Billy Cotton Band Show', in a pantomime or in a summer season show at Blackpool.

After that 1960 tour of the States, Cliff Richard and The Shadows started recording separately as well as together. The Shadows had their first major hit single 'Apache' that year, and a major influence on the embryonic British rock groups – even The Beatles themselves recorded an instrumental number out in Hamburg that they called 'Cry For A Shadow' and which they later acknowledged was Shadows-influenced. They spent nearly six months in a London Palladium stage show 'Stars In Your Eyes' with Russ Conway, Joan Regan and Edmund Hockridge, and maintained their unique run of hit records and TV appearances. Then the following year, with Peter Gormley now Cliff's manager, they really did start to begin consolidating overseas. From this time on, the sure touch of the Gormley-Grade management-agency team was very much evident.

Cliff Richard and The Shadows still continued to make frequent British concert tours, but early that next year (1961) their pace overseas noticeably started to quicken. They made their first tour of South Africa, where vast crowds lined the streets to see them – at that time Cliff and The Shadows probably had a greater following in South Africa than any other act has achieved since. That same year they also appeared in Rhodesia – and Cliff went back to South Africa again at Christmas – and they also toured Australia and New Zealand; appeared in Malaya and Singapore; made concert appearances throughout Scandinavia; starred in a six-week summer season show at Blackpool – and made their first really important film 'The Young Ones', which was to prove a box office success.

Looking back on the year, Cliff told the now-defunct magazine *Hit Parade*: 'I don't mind working hard and long when I feel that I am achieving something – and I really do believe that 1961 has been a particularly good year for me. Not only has it given me the opportunity of getting myself better known in other countries, but the whole scope of my career has broadened . . . I'm told that we registered so favourably (in Australia) that our record sales have now practically doubled there.'

When they arrived in Johannesburg for the first time, a crowd of 3,000 devoted fans had been waiting on the tarmac at the airport to see their plane touch down; more crowds lined the route as they were driven the six miles into the city in a procession of large American cars with a motor cycle escort; their shows were all sold out – and an extra concert was specially arranged for a coloured audience because of the apartheid laws. Wherever they appeared, their schedule was tightly organised with just a few hours for sun-bathing (Bruce Welch received second degree burns in Johannesburg when he exposed himself to the sun too much), or for swimming, or maybe a little sightseeing such as accepting an invitation to a special display of Zulu dancing near Durban.

It was the same story in New Zealand where they worked every day of their ten-day stay – though they did have three days' rest in Singapore as they flew back to London.

The pace was now constant. They were Britain's most successful pop stars with seldom a day to themselves as they arrived back in England to begin rehearsing for 'The Young Ones' before beginning their Blackpool summer show. It was to be the same the following year (1962) as they started the year with Cliff releasing his sixteenth single, two tracks taken from the film (the title track 'The Young Ones' coupled with 'We

Say Yeah') which earned him another Gold Disc for 1,000,000-plus sales. That year they made their second major film 'Summer Holiday' in which they played a group of young people travelling across Europe in a double-decker London bus, ending up in Greece where many of the location scenes were filmed. 'It's a tremendous experience,' Cliff told the *New Musical Express*. 'More so, I'd say, than when I did "The Young Ones". This is because I've now got more confidence in my acting, as well as having a bit more experience in what it's all about . . . it was really fabulous being out in Greece, except that at the time the place was virtually a dust-bowl. The trouble is that they'd been having their August weather a bit too soon, which made it like sitting in an oven on a hot summer's day. I've sunbathed in South Africa and Australia, but this was the first time I'd ever peeled.' When asked about his future plans, he said: 'I'd like to do some straight acting. I'm learning as I'm going along. When I think I've got enough experience I'd like to tackle a dramatic role in a stage play. On the other hand, I'd be tickled pink if I could get away with the kind of suave comedy that Cary Grant does. I've seen a lot of his films and I think he's really great.'

That film proved even more successful than the previous one. Again two tracks were taken from the movie, 'The Next Time' and 'Bachelor Boy', and released as a single in November, 1962, bringing Cliff Richard and The Shadows their third Gold Disc, and an especially important one for Cliff because he had written 'Bachelor Boy' himself with Bruce Welch – the first time he had ever been involved in writing one of his singles. In just over a month that single sold its first 800,000 copies – and by the time the 'Summer Holiday' film was premiered in London and South Africa in January, 1963, the group were again Number 1 in the music paper charts.

There was no doubt now that at that time the group was the most popular that Britain had ever produced. After the box office success of 'The Young Ones' the distributors prepared themselves for the new movie by organising special pre-release showings of 'Summer Holiday' in seventy major British towns and cities – and taking the converted double decker London but with its fitted beds, stove, fridge, bathroom and all home comforts to selected venues so that fans could see for themselves the very bus in which Cliff had been filmed cavorting across Europe. It was high pitch promotion: when the film had its actual premiere, Cliff drove up to the Warner theatre driving that same bus – with an orchestra performing inside the theatre. And then the film went out on general release on February 17th – just as Cliff Richard and The Shadows were beginning a six-week British concert tour supported by Patsy Ann Noble, the Vernon Girls and the Trebletones.

In the intervening weeks, they returned yet again to South Africa appearing in Cape Town on January 16th and then visiting Port Elizabeth, East London, Durban and Johannesburg before going on to Rhodesia for concerts in Bulawayo and Salisbury and then on again to Nairobi in Kenya to attend a charity concert organised by the African leader Tom Mboya.

They were now at their peak and a major entertainment attraction in nearly every country in the world outside the United States. Every week the music papers carried detailed news stories about their future plans. Here are some examples which show how convinced the press were that Cliff Richard fans wanted to know everything about the group:

On January 4th, 1963, the *New Musical Express* reported:

CLIFF RICHARD GOING TO ISRAEL

Cliff Richard and the Shadows will fly to Israel for a ten-day tour in April – almost immediately after finishing their six-week tour of Britain, which starts February 23.

Cliff then plans a short holiday before beginning rehearsals for his long summer season at Blackpool ABC.

On Monday, he filmed a short message for Warner-Pathe to be shown at the South African premiere of his film 'Summer Holiday' which is next Thursday – the same night as it opens in London.

Next week, he films an interview with Peter Haigh for the same film company. The finished result – with a short clipping from 'Summer Holiday' – will be offered to local TV stations in Britain.

On Wednesday, Cliff will be interviewed by David Jacobs in BBC TV's 'Wednesday Magazine'.

Other plans for the gala premiere include a parade of girls in the national costumes featured in the musical. The audience will consist mainly of disc-jockeys, publishers and other figures in the music business.

Five lucky Radio Luxembourg listeners will shortly each be receiving two tickets to the premiere.

They are among contestants in an EMI competition who correctly forecast 'The Next Time' would be higher placed than 'Bachelor Boy' in this week's NME chart.

And then the following week on January 11th, the *New Musical Express* – which was now running a weekly news story on Cliff's career – reported:

CLIFF: NO FILMING TIME THIS YEAR?

Cliff Richard, whose latest screen musical 'Summer Holiday' opened to rave reviews this week when it was premiered in London and South Africa, may not make a film this year.

Producer Kenneth Harper, responsible for 'The Young Ones' and 'Summer Holiday', wants Cliff to make another – but Richard's itinerary does not allow sufficient or suitable time.

Discussions will be held on Cliff's return from his April tour of Israel to see if a solution can be found.

Cliff plans a holiday before starting rehearsals for his summer show at the Blackpool ABC.

'The summer season will run until October, so it is highly unlikely that we will be able to start working then,' said Harper, who has used the past two summers to make films with Cliff.

And then on February 8th, 1963, the *New Musical Express* reported:

CLIFF'S 'TIME-BOY' WAXING SELLS A MILLION!

Cliff Richard has now sold over one million copies of his hit titles, 'The Next Time' and 'Bachelor Boy' based on a combined total of the singles release and the 'Summer Holiday' LP. Cliff and the Shadows, who return from their triumphant South African tour next week, may go back to Scandinavia in April.

British sales of Cliff's current hit single had passed 915,000 on Wednesday. At the same time, sales of the soundtrack album in which it is included reached 95,000. This means that the two hit titles have now sold over one million copies.

Cliff will not qualify for a Gold Disc until the single 'The Next Time'/'Bachelor Boy', has reached the million target.

On the basis of international sales, it is almost certain that this has already happened, but no official announcement can be made until EMI has received sales returns from overseas countries.

This week 'Next Time' hit parade placings abroad, according to 'Billboard' (one of the leading US music trade papers) are Norway (2nd), New Zealand (5th), Denmark (6th) and Hong Kong (8th). 'Bachelor Boy' tops the South African charts and is 8th in Norway.

Speculation is rising as to whether Cliff will qualify for a Gold Disc on the strength of British sales alone. With less than 85,000 sales needed to achieve this target, and both titles still figuring in the Top Twenty, it is very probable.

Richard and the group may make a short tour of Scandinavia in April instead of their projected series of appearances in Israel, which are now likely to fall through.

Copenhagen and Stockholm would be included in the itinerary, starting about April 12 for ten days.

They are returning to Britain from their South African tour next Thursday morning.

As forecast in last weeks NME, Cliff's next single 'Summer Holiday'/'Dancing Shoes' will be released next Friday (15th).

The Shadows' next single, 'Foot Tapper', is now likely to have a different coupling from 'Les Girls' – probably a revival of 'The Breeze and I'. March 1 release is likely.

Carole Grey, Cliff's co-star in 'The Young Ones', and currently touring South Africa with him, will not now be joining his summer show with the Shadows at Blackpool ABC.

The title of the show is 'Holiday Carnival'. After a preview on May 31, it will open on June 1. Cliff and the Shadows are first attraction at the new £300,000 theatre.

News stories like these appeared every week in the music papers throughout 1962 and 1963. Cliff Richard and The Shadows were the biggest names in British pop music. The papers' editors knew that their readers were eagerly following the group's career – and though The Beatles and the other Liverpool groups started their own break-through in the spring of 1963 there was no hint then of the musical revolution to come. For some time yet there was no suggestion that The Beatles might already be out-selling them.

After Cliff Richard and The Shadows returned from South Africa on February 22nd, 1963, the *New Musical Express* reported Cliff as saying: 'The whole tour was quite fantastic. And we did considerably more business than last time we were there. The reception we were given at the various airports was tremendous – particularly at Durban where our arrival coincided with a public holiday . . . the press was very kind to us throughout. Of the nineteen shows we played, we only had one bad review! That was by a Johannesburg critic who thought the whole thing was ridiculous. But another writer in the same city gave us a good write-up, so they cancelled out.'

On Cliff Richard's return from South Africa there had been some criticism in the *Daily Express* by writer Herbert Kretzmer because he had seemed equivocal on the question of apartheid. Kretzmer had said Cliff Richard had an extremely limited knowledge of the subject and had no right to discuss it. Now, Cliff told the *New Musical Express*: 'I agree I'm not qualified to talk about it. We didn't go to South Africa to delve into the racial question. We went there to perform and entertain. But if writers persist in asking me about it, I have to make some comment – even if it's only to brush it aside, because it is not strictly my territory.'

It is only fair to Cliff Richard to say that in those days pop stars were not expected to have any political opinions at all. That, too, changed with The Beatles – who refused to visit South Africa as did many other British

groups. The Beatles also refused to appear in any US city where there were any locally devised racist laws. In a conversation we had some years later, by which time most artistes felt free to express political opinions if they wanted to, Cliff Richard told me bluntly: 'I'm against South Africa's politics - but you find racial prejudice everywhere."

Again, it is only fair to Cliff Richard to point out that in the days when he was Britain's Number 1 recording act, even the music papers seemed unaware that there was a whole generation of young people who took pop music very seriously indeed; who were politically and socially aware, and who were only now beginning to express themselves as a generation. It may seem strange now, but in 1963 a music paper like the *New Musical Express* would report – apparently with a perfectly straight face – that: 'Easter for Cliff Richard will be spent partly at home, and partly in the studio – but, apart from buying his Mum an Easter gift and nibbling a couple of hot cross buns, he will have scarcely any time for relaxation.'

One has to remember all this – because Cliff Richard became a star at a time when the British pop music business was still largely run by agents and managers and record company executives who had no real connection with the music as such; they were usually bald and middle-aged, smoked fat cigars, ate their lunch at Isow's, and still mourned the days of the Music Hall when either they or their friends had been dancers, comedians, music or speciality acts. To them – quite understandably, and this is meant as no criticism whatsoever – pop music was a passing teenage fad. And to them it seemed the most sensible thing in the world that a rising star like Cliff Richard should learn to dance, the skills of choreography and stage presentation – and should be seen to cultivate a personality that was clean-cut and wholesome. To them it would not seem odd that Cliff Richard would talk about buying an Easter gift for his Mum or nibbling his hot cross buns.

But to the teenage rock groups who were only now starting to burst forth from the cellars and coffee bars, who had never considered things like 'image', who had sometimes come close to starving, who had (some of them) played in strip clubs and lived with prostitutes, who had struggled to survive in the seamy corners of the business, Cliff Richard represented all they were fighting against. I don't think he ever realised it – and I am even more certain that it was not his fault.

CHAPTER FOUR

The contrast in background between Cliff Richard and The Shadows and so many of the later British groups who were to take their own music around the world is acute. The difference is basic; Cliff and The Shadows were brought together *after* Cliff had become a pop star – nearly every other major group that was to emerge with the rock boom of the early and mid-Sixties struggled together, often with no change in line-up, frequently for as long as five and sometimes as long as ten years, and almost always against morale-shattering setbacks before *they* became stars themselves.

The Shadows, however, came together originally because Cliff Richard was breaking through with 'Move It' – and he needed a group of musicians to accompany him when appearing live on stage. Thus he employed them – paying them a wage – whereas nearly all the top groups of the Sixties and the Seventies were to be wholly co-operative units, splitting the money that came in equally between them.

Differences like this are fundamental, but again one has to understand that when Cliff Richard started it was the singer who was the star. A group that accompanied a singer was, until The Shadows became successful, no more than three or four musicians brought together maybe for just a tour, or a summer show, paid a weekly wage that might be as low as fifteen to twenty pounds a week each – and quite frequently discarded when the engagement had been fulfilled. It was The Shadows who changed all that. Eventually, they became stars in their own right, recognised as such by audiences, and eventually in 1960 they started recording together *as an instrumental group*, quite separately from Cliff. They were, in fact, Britain's *first* hit group. In the five years from 1960 to 1965, they had twenty hit singles of which five were Number One hits. All of which were recorded *before* The Beatles ever had a major success, and it seems strange now to recall that in the days when Brian Epstein was still working in a shop in Liverpool and managing The Beatles in his spare time he once took John Lennon out for the evening to see the Big Stars who were playing at the Liverpool Empire . . . yes, The Shadows! It is even more ironic that The Shadows made that US tour with Freddie Cannon, Frankie Avalon, Clyde McPhatter, Bobby Rydell and Johnny and the Hurricanes no less than *four years* before The Beatles first visited the United States.

Talking in a reflective mood to the music paper *Melody Maker* in 1973, Shadows guitarist Hank B. Marvin said of that US tour: 'Cliff used to stop the show every night. We'd only do five numbers and we put over a very slick and dynamic stage act. We were still pretty raw, whereas the American scene had left open-necked shirts and things like that behind. America was getting very cool, with artists like Bobby Darin wearing suits and bow ties. To them I suppose we were pretty wild and the kids reacted to it. When we returned we thought we ought to get into the cool business and it resulted in us donning suits and bow ties. We started getting cooler ourselves and that trend lasted in England until The Beatles came along. Cliff and The Shadows should, I believe, have made it in America. When Cliff made the tour he hadn't a record to promote – "Living Doll" had preceded it by about six months. With us, "Apache" was a hit there, but by someone else. In those days, you see, British artistes didn't mean a thing. If we'd had the money to do promotional tours over there, we'd have had plenty of hits I'm sure. We all regret it now but not to the point where we lose sleep over it.'

For many if not most fans, it was Hank B. Marvin's guitar-playing that gave The Shadows their distinctive sound. Although he did not know it then, his success in proving that a boy from a very ordinary background could play the instrument so well was to encourage young musicians all over the country to take up the instrument. Leading guitarists of today like Eric Clapton, Jeff Beck and Jimmy Page all took some of their inspiration from Hank Marvin – and were all to admit as much years later. But, as he said and as I stressed in the last chapter, by the time the beat boom happened in early 1963 Cliff Richard and The Shadows were 'in the cool business'. In that same *Melody Maker* interview, Marvin recalled: 'The Beatles really excited me, because they were so raw. Our coolness was getting too cool, too polished and polite, but they put an end to it. We never thought the Mersey Boom would threaten our position and we didn't feel that we needed to change to cash in on it. I think now that it was probably a mistake. We should have perhaps moved with the trends . . .'

In fact – and in my view this has never been stressed enough – Marvin's contribution to the rock music of today was a crucial one, and his roots were every bit as firmly based in skiffle and rock 'n' roll as those of any of today's superstars. And so were those of his close friend Bruce Welch, whom he has known since their schooldays in Newcastle-upon-Tyne. Like a good number of today's top rock musicians, Marvin and Welch were born early in the Second World War – Marvin on October 28th, 1941, and Welch on November 2nd, 1941. That meant that they were going through grammar school just as the Trad Jazz Boom was at its height in the mid-Fifties and just as Lonnie Donegan was breaking away from jazz with what was soon called skiffle. Donegan's 'Rock Island Line', which started so many teenagers off into making their own music with drums, washboards, tea-chest basses and maybe guitar or banjo was a hit early in 1956 and he was to have twenty-five more hit singles between then and autumn, 1962.

Like teenagers all over the country, Marvin and Welch and their friends at Rutherford Grammar School thought that they, too, could reproduce that skiffle sound. Marvin, whose father was a goods checker on British Railways, had his chance when his French teacher agreed to sell him a second hand banjo for £2.50, while Welch was by then already playing guitar with one of the school's first skiffle groups, The Railroaders. Marvin learned how to play his banjo, started sitting in with the local trad jazz bands and then later joined the Crescent City Skiffle Group – which amalgamated with The Railroaders in 1957. On Marvin's sixteenth birthday his parents gave him a £16.80 Hofner Congress guitar, and within the new group he duly switched to lead guitar while Welch started playing rhythm guitar. This all sounds far more sophisticated than it really was. They were still just an amateur skiffle group, happy to play wherever they could – one of their first gigs was at the Pier Pavilion, a small theatre in South Shields, which was then being run by my father, who used to feature local groups in his Sunday night variety shows. One afternoon Marvin, Welch and the other members of their group turned up and offered to play for free – but my father's conscience got the better of him and he paid them two pounds for the night! Another week, soon after Marvin joined The Railroaders, they appeared for a whole week at the Palace Theatre in Newcastle. But mostly their bookings were in working men's clubs and small ballrooms, where they seldom received more than five pounds a night between them.

In those days, The Railroaders still had a tea-chest bass and a washboard – but those were replaced by a string bass and a drum kit after the group had been down to London and won the first round of a talent contest staged at the Granada cinema in Edmonton. With their new equipment and with Bruce Welch as their vocalist they went down to London again soon after Christmas, 1957, winning the second heat in the talent contest, which gave them a place in the semi-final. By now they had moved away from skiffle and were playing Buddy Holly and Elvis Presley numbers, which brought them bookings nearly every night of the week back in Newcastle. This left them so tired by day that they had both left school, much to the annoyance of their families who felt that they really ought to get themselves a proper job if they were not going to continue their studies.

When the finals of the skiffle contest were staged in April, 1958, Hank and Bruce went down to London – and stayed there.

In the contest itself, The Railroaders came third, and afterwards Marvin and Welch moved into lodgings with a Mrs Bowman as their landlady, and there they stayed for the next eighteen months, sometimes very short of money in the first few weeks, but still very anxious to record together. Like so many other young musicians of the day, when they were not working they would drift down to Soho, and hang around the 21's coffee bar, which was now famous as the place where Tommy Steele had been discovered. Among the people they occasionally used to meet there were Jet Harris, who was later to be bass guitarist with The Shadows, and Tony Meehan, who was later to be their drummer. But back in the early summer of 1958, when The Drifters also used to play occasionally down at the 21's, Marvin and Welch were anxious to get any paid work as musicians they could. One week, Marvin played with another skiffle group The Vipers in Birmingham – and so did Jet Harris. And when another friend of theirs, drummer Pete Chester, formed a group The Chesternuts they played with him, too – it was as two of The Chesternuts that Hank Marvin and Bruce Welch made their television debut in Jack Good's '6.5 Special' TV series.

It was one night that they were playing down at the 21's that Marvin and Welch were first invited to play with Cliff Richard, who had by then already released 'Move It' and had been booked to tour with the Kalin Twins in that October package tour. It was lucky for them that they were – for by a strange coincidence the guitarist who was being sought to accompany Cliff was another of the 21's habituees, none other than Tony Sheridan; yes, the same Tony Sheridan who was later to record with The Beatles out in Hamburg.

But Sheridan did not turn up at all at the 21's that evening – so Hank Marvin was asked whether he would like to join The Drifters for that tour. He said he would – but only if his friend Bruce Welch could join him!

So the Kalin Twins' tour started at the Victoria Hall, Hanley, on October 5th, 1958, with Cliff Richard accompanied by The Drifters – who now comprised his friends Ian Samwell on bass guitar and Terry Smart on drums with Marvin on lead guitar and Welch playing rhythm guitar. Also appearing on that tour was another act, The Most Brothers who were the now internationally-known record producer Mickie Most who was then a singer with his brother David, with their own backing group – which included Jet Harris on bass guitar.

Harris was slightly older than Marvin and Welch, whom he had first met down at the 21's. His real name was Terence Harris and he was born on July 6th, 1939, and brought up in Willesden where his father worked in a factory as a press tool setter. He had been a keen school athlete, even representing Middlesex in the 220 yards on one occasion, and after leaving technical college had become an apprentice sheet metal worker, playing clarinet and later bass guitar in the Soho jazz clubs in the evenings after work. After playing in different clubs, he had eventually given up his factory job to join another backing group – for the pop star Terry Dene, who had three hit records in the late Fifties. He also worked with Don Lang, Wee Willie Harris (with whom he toured for twenty-one weeks in variety) and Tony Crombie's band, before joining The Vipers skiffle group just as skiffle was falling out of fashion. He was still with them, though working intermittently, when the offer came to accompany The Most Brothers on that tour.

On the opening night of the Kalin Twins' tour, Harris stood in the wings at Hanley, listening to Cliff Richard play with The Drifters. Later on in the tour he supplemented them on stage, making the group temporarily a five-piece – and then when the tour was over and Cliff was offered a regular spot in Jack Good's new TV series 'Oh Boy!' and again decided to have a group working with him it seemed the most natural thing to do to send for Jet when Ian Samwell decided he did not want to continue as a musician, but preferred to concentrate on song-writing. ('I left for a simple reason: I wasn't good enough,' Samwell was to later tell the *New Musical Express*.)

So by late November, 1958, The Drifters now comprised Jet Harris on bass guitar, Hank Marvin on lead guitar, Bruce Welch on rhythm guitar – and still Cliff's friend from Cheshunt, Terry Smart, on drums, though he eventually left a few weeks later to join the Merchant Navy which was when Tony Meehan became The Drifters' drummer. That was to be the line-up of Cliff Richard's backing group for the next three years, though their name was soon changed to The Shadows to avoid confusion with the American coloured vocal group. The change in name happened after one of their earliest singles 'Feeling Fine' had been released in the States. When their next single 'Jet Black' was issued in the US they were called The Four Jets, but recording manager Norrie Paramor suggested they needed a better name than that. According to a story in the *New Musical Express*, marking their tenth anniversary in 1968: 'Jet Harris had the brainwave. He and Hank were out on scooters in Ruislip, Middlesex, one day and stopped for a drink. Suddenly, Jet said: "What about The Shadows?" Everyone liked it and in July 1959 that became their new name and has stuck ever since.'

Temporarily, Ian Samwell became their manager; but later they were represented by Peter Gormley, and quickly became much more than just another hired back-up group on a weekly wage. Even before Peter Gormley's involvement, The Shadows had become a top recording act in their own right – 'Apache' brought them their first Number One hit in the summer of 1960 just a few months after they made that American tour.

Until that spring of 1963, The Shadows had no real rivals as Britain's top instrumental group. One hit followed another – 'Man Of Mystery', 'FBI', 'Frightened City', 'Kon-Tiki', 'The Savage', 'Wonderful Land', 'Guitar Tango', 'Dance On', 'Foot-tapper', 'Atlantis' and 'Shindig' during that three year period when every one of their instrumental singles was a Top Ten entry.

As a team, their relationship with Cliff Richard was enough to sell every seat at every theatre in the country – because audiences knew that in their shows The Shadows would have the spot closing the first half of the show, and then they would return again for the top-of-the-bill spot at the end of the concert, backing Cliff Richard. Their popularity was such that even changes in line-up – which were to kill many other groups in the Sixties – made no difference at all to the popularity of The Shadows.

Their live shows then, and I saw them appear with Cliff Richard on several tours, were rather formal in style, with those carefully arranged foot movements, marching to the front of the stage, swinging one leg in an arc around the other, backing again, guitars carving similar patterns; a pattern that was emphasised by their quietly conventional dark suits and discreet shirts and ties (in later years this was even to give way to tuxedos and bow ties). 'Cool' is one word for it; my own impression was that they were being carefully presented in such a way that all generations would find them acceptable.

The first to leave the group was Tony Meehan, who found the pressures of constant travelling, screaming audiences, a heavy schedule of work and very little spare time was not the way he wanted to spend his life. He became a musical director and record producer with Decca in the autumn of 1961, working on such numbers as Louise Cordet's 'I'm Just A Baby', Jay and Tommy Scott's 'Angela' and 'Yuggi Duggi', Garry Mills' 'Never Believed in Love', Michael Cox's 'Honey 'Cause I Love You', Tim Connor's 'Take This Message', and with other musicians like the bandleader Cyril Stapleton, with Ivor Raymonde and with Glyn Johns, later to become known for his own production work with The Rolling Stones and The Who. 'Tony was an amazing drummer. I shall always think that he was the original Keith Moon, because he really used to belt the drums,' Hank Marvin was later to tell *Melody Maker*.

Meehan was replaced by Brian Bennett, who had been in Marty Wilde's backing group The Wilde Cats – and then the following April (1962) Jet Harris, who had always seemed to be the most restless member of the group, also departed to pursue a solo career. Harris first released one solo track 'Theme from "The Man With The Golden Arm"' – and then to many people's surprise teamed up with Tony Meehan, with whom he recorded three very successful singles, 'Diamonds' (which reached Number One in the music paper charts), 'Scarlett O'Hara' (which reached Number Two) and 'Applejack' (Number Four). Within The Shadows, Jet Harris was replaced by Brian 'Licorice' Locking, who stayed with them for eighteen months (until October, 1963) – and then quit so that he could devote more time to his religious work as a Jehovah's Witness. Locking in turn was replaced by John Rostill.

In between times of major upheaval, there were the occasional tremors. In April, 1962, around the time that Harris quit, Bruce Welch was taken ill at a concert in Blackpool, where he collapsed on stage, and was temporarily replaced by guitarist-songwriter Peter Carter. Eighteen months later, again troubled by ill-health, Welch announced that he was leaving but then later changed his mind. Much later still, Welch did leave The Shadows and was replaced by Alan Hawkshaw. For nearly two years Welch ran the group's music publishing companies, and for a while also co-managed with Gormley an Australian group The Virgil Brothers. But Marvin and Welch remained close as they had already been, and later invited the Australian musician John Farrar to England to join them in the trio Marvin, Welch and Farrar. Then more recently The Shadows as such re-formed (in the autumn of 1974) now comprising Marvin, Welch, Farrar and Brian Bennett, and represented Britain in the Eurovision Song Contest in March, 1975, when they came second with the number 'Let Me Be The One'.

The most tragic story of all was that of Jet Harris. As I mentioned earlier, he had always seemed more restless than the others; when I first saw the group performing with Cliff Richard I can remember that off-stage he dressed differently, and was clearly excitable and highly strung. He would become very nervous before a show, not that that in itself is unusual; even Cliff himself has been known to be physically sick just before a show, and even John Lennon, so often thought to be such a strong character, has been sick with nerves before a live appearance. But poor Jet Harris really was nervy – and had the most rotten bad luck.

At the time that he left The Shadows, he had a devoted fan following; on stage he seemed a natural extrovert, playing to the audience – and yet at the same time managing to be slightly withdrawn. If the truth be known, he probably needed the security of being part of a well-managed, well-protected group – but Jet wanted something different. He wanted to be a solo star, appearing on stage, with a group backing *him* – and when he went solo that was what he set out to achieve. But by then his first marriage had already collapsed, and – as he later admitted telling his life story to *The People* – he was already drinking heavily.

After leaving The Shadows in April, 1962, Harris spent some months rehearsing in a central London studio; released that one solo single 'Theme from "The Man With The Golden Arm"' (also referred to in some reference works as 'Main Title Theme') which was a minor hit, as was the coupling 'Some People' on which he made his debut as a solo vocalist. Harris than made his first solo stage appearance at Torquay's Princess Theatre on August 19th. So far as many fans were concerned, Jet was already a major star in his own right even before he made that solo debut. His new manager Roy Moseley told the *New Musical Express*: 'His fan mail is so big the GPO deliver it to my office separately each day – in a sack. Fans besiege my office from all over the country in search of him. It's been necessary to keep him under cover all these months. The emphasis has been on work – hard work . . .' Both Jet Harris's performances at Torquay sold out, and he was subsequently booked to appear with a backing group The Jetblacks on an autumn tour of Britain supporting the American rock star Little Richard, and sharing second billing with Sam Cooke.

Later that autumn Harris, by now playing guitar instead of

bass, recorded 'Diamonds' with Tony Meehan – which to their astonishment turned out to be a Number One hit. 'We looked upon it as a one-shot novelty, and we didn't dream that it would be such a success. Now we're determined to carry on together . . . quite frankly, neither of us imagined that we'd be teaming up together. We were each cherishing big plans for ourselves individually, but they've gone by the board now,' Harris told the *New Musical Express.*

As a double act with a backing group, Jet Harris and Tony Meehan started appearing together in concert and on TV; they released two further hit singles during 1963 'Scarlett O'Hara' and 'Applejack'; released two EPs and an LP, and made a nationwide tour – but Jet Harris just seemed to be accident prone. Everything went wrong for him.

When they appeared together at the *New Musical Express* annual Poll Winners' Concert, which was then the biggest event of the year in the music business, it was Tony Meehan who fell over as they left the stage; his foot caught in a wire leading to one of the amplifiers on the platform. 'I fell flat on my face in front of 10,000 people – and it took two attendants nearly a minute to extricate me,' he said afterwards.

But mostly it was Jet Harris who had the bad luck. He was injured in a car crash in July, 1963 – and was injured again in another car crash in September, 1963, when he was travelling with his girlfriend singer Billie Davis in a chauffeur-driven hired car that was in collision with a bus near Evesham. By the time of the accident, Jet Harris and Tony Meehan were again in the charts with their third hit 'Applejack' – but that was to prove the last of their hit records.

In December, 1966, Jet Harris was awarded £11,150 for his injuries in the car crash in an action against the Birmingham and Midland Omnibus Company and against the driver of the bus, who both denied negligence. 'Although he was no Beatle and possibly no Cliff Richard, he was nevertheless at the top of his profession,' said the judge, Mr Justice Donaldson, when the case was brought before the High Court.

In the intervening years, Jet Harris appeared in court several times. His romance ended with Billie Davis, who nursed him through the period after the second crash. 'It is just impossible for me to stay with Jet,' she told *The Daily Sketch.* 'He so desperately needs someone to be with him all the time and I have tried hard to help him. But he won't listen . . . Jet is a very difficult person to control, but he has been very good all the time he was working. I hate doing this but I have tried with him for well over a year and now I am convinced that it just could not have worked out.' In another interview, Billie Davis said that Jet had had to have twenty stitches in his scalp after the accident, and would say: 'Look at my hands. I can't stop them shaking. I can't eat and I've got this migraine. The thought of going on stage petrifies me . . .'

Only three weeks after the crash, Jet Harris and Tony Meehan had been due to appear on what was then the top British TV pop series, Rediffusion's 'Ready, Steady Go!' to promote 'Applejack'. And just before the show was due to go on the air, Jet vanished from the studio. He subsequently said in that series in *The People*: 'Although my head was shaved, showing a mauve scar, and my body and hands were still so bruised I couldn't possibly have played a guitar properly, the fans expected me to appear. For a week before the show I worried myself sick at the thought of it. On the actual day I found my nerves had snapped completely. My hands were shaking so much I couldn't get a match to a cigarette in my mouth. My head was twitching violently and my vocal chords locked in a hopeless stammer the moment I tried to say anything. In a trance I caught a cab to the television studios and tried to hide myself in a corner of the dressing room which seemed packed with people. For thirty minutes I just sat there watching the minutes tick by on the dressing room clock, knowing that I couldn't possibly appear before the television cameras. Then when the programme was about to begin I suddenly threw myself through the door, down the corridor, past the commissionaire at the front door and into the first cab I saw. When the programme went on the air, Tony had to apologise to the millions of viewers waiting for our latest number together. I don't quite know where I went that night. But eventually Billie found me hiding at a friend's flat in Brighton and began nursing me and trying to restore my shattered nerves . . .'

Over the years that followed both before the settlement of the damages action and afterwards, he was to appear before different courts. He was divorced by his first wife, Carol Ann;

then later Billie Davis broke off their engagement; in June, 1966, by which time Jet was working as a barman at the Tankard and Castle public house in Cheltenham, he married Christina Susan Speed, who was working as a hotel assistant. After the wedding Jet told the London *Evening Standard*: 'All I want to do at the moment is to settle down and be a normal married man. But I hope to start making records again soon.' But before the end of the year his second wife had started divorce proceedings. At other times he appeared in court on drinking-and-driving charges, for possessing cannabis and the drug LSD and on a charge of common assault – and was said to have undergone psychiatric treatment.

Within the music business, many people tried to help him. At one stage he went into business with Lord Lichfield; both of them were connected with a company that was managing the groups Platform Six and The Idols. 'My main activity will be to photograph the artists,' said Lord Lichfield. The Rolling Stones' guitarist Brian Jones helped to write a song for Jet Harris, and the Stones' own record producer Andrew Oldham produced a recording session for him. And after that second marriage, Cliff Richard bought him bass and lead guitars, amplifiers and a fuzz box costing in total £700 to help Harris get started again in the business. (Only a few months earlier in December, 1965, Cliff had said in an interview with the *Melody Maker*: 'I haven't seen Jet for years, but I must say he's been quite a disappointment for me. When he left us, he and Tony Meehan made a couple of great records and we thought, great, there'll be some great instrumentals coming out. Such a shame . . .')

After receiving the new equipment, Harris told *The Daily Express*: 'I have always wanted to make a come-back with a group but I have not been exactly well off . . . the last thing I want to do is to rush things and have another nervous break-down.' Now Tony Meehan stepped in again, and produced a come-back record for Harris – 'My Lady', written by Reg Presley of The Troggs. 'You know I owe everything to Tony. I reckon he's a bit of a genius on the quiet,' Harris was quoted as saying in a press release from Fontana Records to promote the record. Of the recording session itself, he said: 'Going in there and seeing those session men and having no part to play from, I thought they would all be looking at me, but after the first run-through I forgot my nerves and just started enjoying myself . . . I've had enough of the limelight. In future, I just want to be a bass player, doing my job as well as I can.' Even sadder was a comment he made in an interview with *Melody Maker* just as the record was released: 'I wanted to forget pop entirely for a while, but three years is a long time to be away. I was turning into a fossil and I felt very depressed. I worked as a barman and as a labourer. I was used to a thousand pounds a week then I was down to nine pounds labouring on the roads . . .'

But the record failed. Two years later, it was reported that Jet Harris was joining a group in Nottingham; later still he was found to be working for a bus company . . .

To fail in the music business is sad enough, but in the case of Jet Harris I have always felt that he was a musician ahead of his time who knew in his bones that the music was changing. When Cliff Richard and The Shadows were first starting he was as much a heart-throb in his way as Cliff Richard was but more lean-featured, hungry-looking. By the time he left the group, he was without a doubt one of the better guitarists that the business had produced, with a clear instinct that his direction had to change. In a recent interview with *Radio Times*, Jerry Lordan who wrote that first hit for The Shadows – 'Apache' – said: 'The Shadows made it big everywhere else (except the States), with the guys in the audience watching how Hank played his guitar and the girls looking at moody Jet Harris whom they loved. A kind of forerunner of Brian Jones, was Jet. And in that same article, Cliff Richard commented: 'All the guys related to Hank Marvin and all the girls to Jet Harris.' And Tony Meehan said: 'The band I formed with Jet Harris, who was just the best guitarist around, played the way I felt The Shadows ought to play. I thought The Shadows should have gone in the direction the Meehan/Harris band went with "Scarlett O'Hara" and "Diamonds". At that time, The Shadows, like everyone else in pop, thought they were there forever. The Beatles were a complete shock to us all. What was new about them was that they weren't showbizzy. I think they took the wind out of our sails . . .' In music and even in matters like image, Jet Harris was ahead of so many other musicians of that time. Once The Beatles had arrived and so many other groups had become successful in their wake, Hank Marvin said a little sadly to the *Evening Standard*: 'You know those moody pictures, all black and gloomy, that they all have taken nowadays? Well, we wanted to have those. Jet was always wanting to have his picture taken with the glass of whisky and the cigarette but they wouldn't let him. Bad for the image, they said. It annoys us a bit really. Our old photographs looked like those old bandleaders with the grin. The sort that make you laugh and say: "Look at those lapels."'

CHAPTER FIVE

To put it at its simplest, both Cliff Richard and The Shadows found themselves stuck with an image in 1963 that became quickly out of date – and it is my own view that if this had not happened they would almost certainly have become one of the most successful British groups ever to appear in the United States. As it was, they were still at the top of the local charts in nearly every other country in the world. Their success had reached a peak with no parallel in the history of the British music business. There seemed no reason why Cliff Richard and The Shadows could not go on for ever; their position as the country's Number One group seemed almost unchallengeable.

And then The Beatles happened, rocketing to Number One with every single they released – and their music was fresh, bold and different.

At first, the contrast was not all that apparent – to begin with The Beatles were quite conventional in appearance, dressed in their Pierre Cardin suits, with their 'mop top' haircuts and high heeled black boots. They were every bit as image-conscious as Cliff Richard and The Shadows – John Lennon even kept his marriage to Cynthia and the fact that he was a father secret for some months, and would not dream of appearing in public with glasses even though he could hardly see without them.

But the mood of the country was changing. It was one of those strange periods in the history of British entertainment when the theatre, television and even pop music seemed to reflect a sudden shift in popular thinking; as is so often the case this shift occurred long before the politicians or the press realised it. In the theatre, the satirical revues had been poking fun at the establishment – and now there was even a club in Soho called The Establishment where the American comedian Lenny Bruce was being viciously anarchic nightly. In television, audiences of as many as 12,000,000 people would sit up late on a Saturday night to watch 'That Was The Week That

Was' which brilliantly satirised the weaknesses of a Government that was almost visibly falling to pieces. The magazine 'Private Eye' was beginning to print the sort of stories that the Press had long been afraid to touch; the Profumo Scandal was shaking the Establishment to its foundations; there was a feeling in the country that after twelve years of Conservative Government the time had come for a change; there were violent political swings of opinion in the by-elections . . . and in the music business along came The Beatles, who were fresh, anti-establishment, ever-so-slightly-outrageous, and who quickly captured the mood of the nation.

The country's teenagers like their parents were in a mood for something new. And The Beatles gave it to them – as did all the other groups who came scurrying from The Cavern and Liverpool's other clubs and coffee bars; who came hurrying down to London from Birmingham, Manchester and Newcastle-Upon-Tyne, buying their guitars and amplifiers as fast as the hire purchase companies would let them.

Within the music business, a revolution was happening – but few people realised it. Cliff Richard did not realise it. The Shadows did not know. But that was no reflection on them – the press and television companies did not know either. The old established agents and managers carried on arranging their summer shows and pantomimes, not realising that what the teenagers wanted was live music in their own towns. It was to be a full six months before the news started to break through in Fleet Street.

Having started the year the undisputed top pop group in the land, Cliff Richard and The Shadows continued their own sweet way.

That Easter, in that same *New Musical Express* story that talked of his gift for his Mum and his hot cross buns, Cliff talked of the TV special he was planning to record in April; of his two forthcoming albums (one of them a collection of past hits), and the 16-week summer show at Blackpool in which he was due to star with The Shadows. 'Believe me, I'm really going to enjoy the summer show, as The Shadows and I will be working all the way through it – in sketches and production numbers, as well as our own spots. One sequence which I can't wait to see is a comedy adagio routine, in which The Shadows get involved with the dancers and find themselves hurled all over the stage!'

When Cliff Richard and The Shadows went to Spain to record in Barcelona, the *New Musical Express* duly reported that they had eaten asparagus tips, steaming hot fish soup 'and other Spanish delicacies – plus a large jug of red wine'. It talked of Cliff 'listening rapturously to an album by the great Spanish guitarist, Segovia'; and informed their fans that Cliff and The Shadows had duly shouted 'Ole!' when they visited a bull fight in Barcelona. ('You certainly wouldn't call it a sport,' said Cliff. 'I'm glad I went – but I wouldn't want to go to another.')

When The Shadows appeared with him at that Blackpool summer show, Cliff told the readers of *Hit Parade*: 'We do have lots of fun together, off-stage as well as on, and apart from anything else, I'm intending to indulge in a lot of sun-bathing and photography sessions during the next few months . . .' In August, it was reported that he had been voted 'most promising singer' in a nation-wide ballot by the American teen magazine '16' – and that he had entered the *Billboard* chart with 'Lucky Lips', his first American chart entry since 'Living Doll' in 1959. The following week *The New Musical Express* reported that 'Lucky Lips' had reached Number 89 (yes, 89) in the *Billboard* chart. The story read:

> CLIFF TOPS SIX OVERSEAS CHARTS IN A WEEK!
>
> Cliff Richard, who will be seen receiving his third Gold Disc on tomorrow's edition of 'Lucky Stars Summer Spin' is currently topping the charts in six foreign countries – an unprecedented achievement for a British artist. He is now expected to film his edition of the Ed Sullivan US TV show here on September 22.
>
> Cliff received the Gold Disc for a million sales of his 'Bachelor Boy'/'The Next Time' single from recording manager Norrie Paramor during the telerecording of ABC TV's 100th 'Luck Stars' show on Sunday and it is included in tomorrow's programme screening.
>
> Cliff's six round-the-world chart-topping positions are all with 'Lucky Lips' – an outstanding achievement for the disc

that failed to make the number one spot in Britain!

In 'Billboard's' world-wide chart reports, it is the best seller in Norway, Israel, South Africa, Hong Kong, Sweden and Holland, where his 'Summer Holiday' gives him a second Top Ten placing at number eight.

In America, 'Lucky Lips' has climbed six places this week to the 89 spot in the Hot 100.

As previously reported, famous American TV personality Ed Sullivan is filming two of his shows in London – with Cliff and The Shadows starring in one and Frank Ifield in the other.

Latest development is that both shows will almost certainly be filmed on the same day – Sunday, September 22 – with Cliff and The Shadows dashing to London directly after their Blackpool show the previous evening.

That same month Cliff Richard celebrated his fifth anniversary as a recording artist, and commenting on the success of his records overseas the *New Musical Express* writer Derek Johnson said: 'One of the reasons why Cliff's efforts reap such an abundant reward abroad, particularly on the Continent, is that he goes to great lengths to record in the specific language of the market he is attacking. His latest move in this direction is to record 'Lucky Lips' in German. "It's all done phonetically," he assured me. "I never have the slightest idea what I'm singing about! I find it extremely easy to get to grips with Spanish and French, because they are both essentially musical languages. German is very gutteral and much more difficult to master."'

The following month, after reports in the national press that there was a developing romance between himself and the dancer Jackie Irving (who was to later marry Adam Faith), Cliff told the *New Musical Express*: 'It's true that I've taken Jackie out more than any other girl. But then, being placed as I am, it's only natural that I should take out girls I know, rather than those I don't know. Jackie and I have been thrown together professionally quite a lot and I've grown to know her pretty well. I enjoy her company very much, but I can assure you that we've never even discussed the possibility of marriage – except, perhaps, to the contrary. Jackie's a good pal and we're the best of friends. But the chances are, now that the

Blackpool season is over I shan't see her again for a few months. And that hardly indicates romance, does it?'

The romance finished soon afterwards, and although it is the only time that Cliff Richard has been publicly linked with a girlfriend it was not the first; he once told me that he regretted 'a great deal' the fact that he had broken off another romance earlier in his career. 'It dates back to the time I was just breaking into pop,' he said. 'I had a steady girlfriend, and had taken her out for quite a time. My one and only teenage romance. But then, when things started going well for me, I decided that a girlfriend would be bad for my image and broke it off. It was a mistake and I have regretted it ever since. We both got over it all right. In fact, she is happily married now.' He refused to say who the girl was. 'That stays a secret,' he said. 'But if the same thing were to happen now, I would go ahead and marry the girl. I don't believe it is harmful nowadays for a pop star to get married.'

In October 1963, Cliff Richard and The Shadows toured Israel – and then started work on their third major film 'Wonderful Life', in which their co-star was Susan Hampshire. 'One of the biggest disappointments of my film career was watching "Wonderful Life" for the first time,' Cliff later told *Melody Maker*. 'When we did it we thought "this is going to be the best film." But when we saw it cut together, something was lacking, there was no continuity in the story, but I'll still say, subject matter-wise, it was the best thing I've ever done. For me anyway.'

The image that seemed to be developing even more strongly throughout 1963 was almost incredibly boyish – at a time when the music business was becoming much more masculine and aggressive. And then there was the fact that he seemed to be becoming even more of an Establishment-figure at a time when this was no longer the vogue – and the fact that he could talk in almost twee terms about his romance with Jackie Irving at a time when the groups that had emerged from the North were rampaging around the country in a continuing story of drunken decadence (which is best left undescribed here). To put it bluntly, his image was out of date – and this was further emphasised by the fact that when The Beatles and many of the other emerging groups were still living mainly at home in their Northern council estates, Cliff Richard went out and bought a palatial house called Rookswood at Nazeing in Essex, with six bedrooms, four bathrooms and a billiards room. The London *Evening Standard* reported: 'It has a patio at one end with stone pillars on either side; a beautiful rose garden. The house stands in eleven acres of ground with a 300-yard long drive. The garage can accommodate four or five cars. There are greenhouses and stabling. The house stands on high ground overlooking Hoddesdon Common. It has a splendid view of the Lea Valley looking towards London. Inside there is a large hall panelled in oak from Hampton Court. The main lounge, which has a light-coloured decor, has a fine Adams-type fireplace in white. The oak-panelled dining-room is Elizabethan in style, with candelabra over the white marble fireplace. On the second floor is a master bedroom with bay mullioned windows and inbuilt furniture. The room has delicately painted white and pink wood. A curtained-off bathroom adjoins it. The whole house is centrally heated. A feature of the grounds is a wooded glen with a water glen and 40 foot waterfall. Cliff and his mother, Mrs Dorothy Webb, moved in last Friday.' To the *New Musical Express*, Cliff said: 'We won't have a live-in maid, just a daily, so I am converting it (the maid's apartment). I am getting a super tape recorder like Hank's and I have already got a machine that makes master records – so maybe I'll make hits at home, like I have read Chet Atkins does in Nashville.' Asked whether he thought the house might not be too large for him and his mother, Cliff Richard said: 'No, it has only one bedroom more than our last place and she never complained there. And my sisters, who continue to go to school at Cheshunt each day, help. Mother and I looked at loads of houses. We nearly settled for one at Radlett but finally took the Nazeing house. We bought it a year ago and have just recently moved in . . .'

In all, the mock-Tudor style house had eighteen rooms and had cost him £30,000. He spent another £2,000 laying out tennis courts. And soon afterwards bought himself a holiday home in Albufeira, Portugal, as well. He was clearly already a wealthy man. When he moved less than three years later, Cliff was able to sell the house for £43,500 – and that was long before the great boom in property prices. Today such a home could possibly cost around £150,000.

For most of his fans, living on council estates or in modest semi-detached homes, Cliff Richard was fast becoming remote and even more typically 'show-biz' – just at the very time that the music business itself was becoming 'anti-show-biz' with The Beatles stressing their very ordinariness; with dozens of other groups amplifying the same impression, and with fans all over Britain expecting the top groups of the day to turn up at the local town halls and city ballrooms squashed into their second hand vans, with their road manager at the wheel, and all their precious equipment stacked in the back.

Whereas Cliff Richard and The Shadows would star in a sixteen-week Blackpool summer show, record in Spain or fly to different parts of the world to make their latest film or star in 'Sunday Night At The London Palladium', the groups that were storming the charts that year were on a never-ending cycle of one-nighters, appearing in Bolton one night, Blackburn the next, followed by Manchester, Wigan, Leeds or Burnley – and before the shows their fans would often help carry the equipment into the ballroom.

Looking back now, it is astonishing that Cliff Richard and The Shadows managed to survive.

But they did – even though The Shadows were never to have another Number One single, and it was to be two years before Cliff Richard himself returned to the Number One slot himself with his single 'The Minute You're Gone'. By the time he did in March, 1965, The Beatles had broken through in the United States and all around the world, and so had other groups in their wake like The Dave Clark Five, Herman's Hermits, Gerry and the Pacemakers, Billy J. Kramer and the Dakotas, Wayne Fontana and the Mindbenders, The Zombies and The Rolling Stones.

In those intervening years, The Shadows and Cliff Richard were still successful in their own way; they appeared in their stage shows and Christmas pantomime; their next film was another box office success; overseas they now had a loyal following, and though they might not be million-sellers every record they released was still a chart entry, much of the material now being written by either Hank Marvin or Bruce

Welch. Cliff also recorded outstanding songs by other writers, such as 'It's All In The Game', which had been a Number One hit in November, 1958, for Tommy Edwards and 'Blue Turns To Grey', which was written by Mick Jagger and Keith Richard of The Rolling Stones – but to me this seemed to accentuate the difference between his position as an established 'all round entertainer' and the newly emerging groups who tended to write all their own material.

Cliff's image, whether intentional or not, was still very innocent, in that third major film with The Shadows, 'Wonderful Life', Susan Hampshire gave him his first screen kiss. 'I liked it. Susan is a crazy, marvellous girl and makes a wonderful leading lady,' he told the magazine *Hit Parade*, apparently unaware that the fans of 1963 might find it rather odd that a top star could reach the age of twenty-three without being publicly kissed! Again it was probably just bad luck that he should be making another teenage pop film just as The Beatles were about to give a fatal kick to that genre, too, with their vastly superior movie 'A Hard Day's Night'.

In 'The Young Ones', he had played the son of a property developer who found that his father's business plans might lead to the destruction of the local youth club; in 'Summer Holiday' he was seen romping through Europe in a double-decker bus, moving from one song-and-dance routine to the next – and now in 'Wonderful Life', which was largely filmed on location in the Canary Islands, he played a stunt man with a film unit who decided to make his own film with a group of friends plus Susan Hampshire. Thus in one film scene Cliff portrayed Groucho Marx and in another Errol Flynn; The Shadows appeared as US Marines capturing Burma; in another scene Cliff Richard was seen riding a camel – and in another he was shown wrestling in a swamp with a 30ft long crocodile, while Hank Marvin appeared as Tarzan wrapped in a loin-cloth (still with his spectacles on, of course!), and in yet another sequence The Shadows appeared in evening dress as part of a small orchestral group. It was all harmless fun. Young children probably loved it, and it was the sort of film their parents could take them to without being worried – but by then the audiences that Cliff Richard had first started playing to in 1958 and 1959 were in their late teens and early twenties, adults themselves and looking for something more mature.

In every way, Cliff Richard and The Shadows seemed to be hardly changing while all around them was in a state of turmoil and eager excitement as pop music extended its frontiers, and moved out of the town hall ballrooms and into the vast city stadiums of Europe and the United States, becoming the biggest money-spinner in international show business since the invention of the Talkies.

But Cliff Richard still had a large audience of his own; there were (and always will be) parents who want to take their children to a summer show when on Holiday in Blackpool, who enjoy Christmas pantomimes and seasonal productions, who are reassured to know that there are innocuous film musicals for their teenaged daughters to watch and who do themselves enjoy sharing such experiences, and listening to ballads and other songs that are easy on the ear.

Yes, Cliff Richard and The Shadows had become Family Entertainers – while at the same time retaining a large teenage following which might not have been as huge as that of The Beatles, The Rolling Stones and the other groups that were emerging, but which was nevertheless considerable, both in Britain and in other parts of the world.

After completing the 'Wonderful Life' film early in 1964 they went on to tour Holland, Belgium, Germany, France and again Scandinavia.

A correspondent reported to the *New Musical Express* from Copenhagen in Denmark: 'I must admit I have never seen a Danish audience go wild like it did in the packed, 2,000 seater Falke-theatre during the second of his two shows on Wednesday. When Cliff asked the audience to sing 'The Young Ones' with him, the 2,000 teenagers sang along with him as one – in English, of course, because pop songs have helped Danes to speak English! Later they belted out 'yeah, yeah' during Cliff's 'We Say Yeah' and went completely wild! At the end the crowd rushed down on to the stage and tried to climb on to it, to be thrown back by attendants and police. For nearly 45 minutes after the show, the audience refused to leave and shouted 'We want Cliff'. So successful was the visit, Cliff and

The Shadows are re-booked to Copenhagen on Monday for another two concerts, unscheduled before he came here.' From Helsinki, Finland, it was reported that Cliff Richard and The Shadows had 'made a sensational appearance . . . driving thousands of teenagers wild with excitement.' In Stockholm, there was said to have been 'thunderous applause' at the end of each number.

After appearing in another summer show that year – this time at Great Yarmouth ABC – the group toured Britain in the autumn; starred in the Royal Variety Show, and then opened in pantomime at the London Palladium just before Christmas in 'Aladdin and his Wonderful Lamp' with Arthur Askey and Una Stubbs, and a musical score written specially for the production by The Shadows themselves.

This was their second pantomime and their second season at the London Palladium; their first pantomime was at the Stockton Globe, when they opened just before Christmas, 1959 – and the group had appeared in that summer revue at the Palladium in 1960. But with The Shadows having written the music, and with numbers like 'Genie With The Light Brown Lamp' and 'I Could Easily Fall' soon entering the music paper charts this was a much more important production – and a great box office success. Even while the show was still running, Cliff Richard returned to Number One in the charts again for the first time in two years with the song 'The Minute You're Gone', which he had recorded during a brief visit to Nashville the previous summer.

'I haven't been bored once during the entire run,' he told the *New Musical Express*. 'And that's due almost entirely to the wonderful company working with me. We've had a lot of fun, and we've kept in good spirits by having one party after another. Every show has been interesting, mainly because something different has happened at each performance . . . all the same, I can't say that I'm sorry it's ending. It isn't because I'm fed up with the show. It's simply that I'm looking forward to all the other things that are pending for me.'

While Cliff Richard and The Shadows were still appearing nightly at the Palladium, there was public confirmation that he was now a wealthy man – with reports in the national press that he and Frank Ifield (who was then also managed by Peter

Gormley) had collected £474,000 by selling shares in their private companies to Constellation Investments. 'Most of the money is likely to go to 24-year-old Cliff Richard in a deal which almost certainly establishes him as a millionaire,' reported *The Daily Express.* The London *Evening Standard* reported: 'A "popularity" clause has been worked into the deals between Constellation Investments and singer Cliff Richard and Frank Ifield. This protects the company against any falling off in the estimated earnings of the two singers. Part of the £73,000 worth of Convertible debenture will be "held back" or rather, will not carry full conversion rights. If profits don't come up to expectations, then some part of the Convertible debenture will be cancelled. Constellation has bought Cliff Richard's Minstrel Enterprises, which owns the exclusive rights to all his live stage performances and two companies from Frank Ifield. This is the first time it's been possible to buy shares in a company which owns pop star rights. Efforts by others to cash in on the popularity of well-known names have run up against problems. One of them is that most investors are reluctant to back the chance that a given pop singer will stay in the top money earning bracket for years to come. The agreement between the company and the two singers seems to have overcome this objection . . .'

The news was a sensation in all the national papers, though in fact the Cliff Richard earnings that were now being partly revealed were only a fraction of those that were being amassed by The Beatles, who had now broken through sensationally in the United States. Interviewed by *The Daily Express*, Cliff Richard said: 'Surely it takes more than I've done to be a millionaire . . . me a millionaire? Can't believe it really, what with all the tax and that. I know I could retire. I never worry about money. I know my manager Peter Gormley isn't going to let me down.' He said that when his accountant had first looked at his finances five years earlier, he had said: 'That's it boy. You're bankrupt!' 'Now he pays all my bills. I just sign for things. If we've got a bit extravagant he starts saying: "Hey, boys, pull your horns in!"' And Peter Gormley himself commented: 'Cliff doesn't know anything about the financial side of things, you know.'

During 1965, Cliff Richard and The Shadows toured Britain

again; filmed three hour-long television shows for ATV; made another major Continental tour – and then in October made their first appearance behind the Iron Curtain, with four concerts in Warsaw at the request of the Polish Government, before flying on to the Lebanon for three days of concert appearances in Beirut.

After returning from the tour, Cliff told the *Sunday Mirror*: 'We went to Poland . . . because they were showing our film "The Young Ones" in Warsaw. I knew that because of currency difficulties it's impossible to buy my discs in the Eastern bloc so I more or less expected to creep in and out. There were 15,000 fans at the airport to greet us. But what amazed me most is that whereas in the West fans are nearly always youngsters, there about half of the crowd who twice crashed the barriers could have been mums and dads. It was the same at concerts. At the end of a number Poles don't scream. Instead, they cheer – a great big booming sound that's staggering.' Asked about the security regulations, he said: 'If there's an Iron Curtain, all I can say is that it must have been in for repairs. Somebody took our passports and gave them back later. In Warsaw, we went where we wanted. It was as easy-going as walking along Bond Street . . . although they can't buy the discs they listen to Radio Luxmbourg and the BBC. People talk to me about politics when I've visited various countries. For instance after I went to South Africa a journalist asked me about political conditions there. When I told him I didn't see anything he said I was a "blind young berk". Maybe I am – but I'm supposed to be in the entertainment business, not in politics.' (Some time later he commented to me that he noticed 'a curious greyness' about the people he saw walking along the street while in Warsaw.)

By then Cliff Richard's lifestyle was already such that he was able to pace himself, and take regular holidays, frequently at that other home he owned in Portugal. He described Albufeira as a fishing village, sun drenched, with a beach that was fanned by cool breezes coming in from the Atlantic. 'When I'm there I lead a life that is quite different from the one I have for the rest of the year,' he told me, adding that the house was small and semi-detached, one of a block of six. He said that Frank Ifield had the adjoining house, and that his manager Peter Gormley and Bruce Welch of The Shadows were neighbours, and so was his agent Leslie Grade, who had bought two houses in the block, combining them into one. He added that actress Muriel Young (now a highly successful pop TV producer) lived nearby, and that William Rushton was a frequent visitor to the area.

'My first job when I bought it was to furnish the house,' he told me. 'This was wonderful fun. I kept the living room sparse; it's so hot in Portugal that you only need light furniture ... I decorated the room with a floral pattern on a black wood background, bringing in a suite that had been made locally in leather, with a straw-topped table, and a green carpet ... I felt that I didn't need too much furniture in the house because the main reason for going over there is to use the house as a base so that I can spend most of the time sunbathing on the beach, swimming, or dining out with friends – I quite often make friends out there who have nothing whatsoever to do with the music business ... one year I met a party of students on the beach, who spoke Portugese and French as well as English, and we went round the restaurants in the evenings, dancing to local rock 'n' roll groups, without anyone treating me as a star ... there's a nice, friendly atmosphere in the clubs out there, where you all sit around, eating and drinking, dancing together, and trying the local wines which are marvellous.'

Although he was now an international star with a following very different from that of so many of the then currently popular British groups, it became clear throughout 1965 that Cliff Richard was becoming restless and was beginning to think about his future; although this was not generally known at the time, he had been becoming more and more interested in religion – particularly since the death of his father in May, 1961. His father had been a major influence on him, hiring and firing managers on his behalf, and gently guiding him in his early years in the music business. I once asked Cliff Richard what had been the most sensible advice his parents had ever given him, and he had replied: 'I think it was when I first came into show business and my father saying: "Learn to be satisfied with what happens ... be prepared for not being the greatest thing in show business. It doesn't matter." That has helped me to take the disappointments – and I still get them.' He was to say years later in that interview with *The Daily Telegraph* supplement that: 'I admired him, but until about the time of his death we were never very close. When he was very ill we got on better. I suppose I looked stronger to him.'

Some time after his father had died, Licorice Locking – a devout Jehovah's Witness – joined The Shadows and during a tour of Australia when they were confined to their hotel rooms for much of the time, he and Cliff Richard used to spend hours discussing religion. Every night they would read the Bible, and for two years thereafter Cliff himself thought quite seriously of becoming a Jehovah's Witness himself. 'I was sure he was right,' Cliff told *The Daily Telegraph.* And so were other people in his family circle and among his closest friends – his sister Jacqueline became a member of the Jehovah's Witnesses, and his mother and his other two sisters, Jan and Donna, 'remained so unofficially'. (When I asked him about his Christmas plans some time, Cliff said he could not give presents to his sisters who were Jehovah's Witnesses because they did not believe in celebrating Christmas by exchanging gifts.)

In the end, Cliff did *not* become a member of the sect – and very few people outside his immediate circle knew how seriously he had considered the decision. (Another of his close friends, Hank Marvin, did join the Jehovah's Witness movement.) But it became apparent during 1965 that his attitudes were changing in many ways; this was something that emerged from different interviews. While he was still appearing in that London Palladium pantomime, he told the magazine *Rave*: 'I have changed a lot in my attitude to work. I have become more and more serious about it . . . I think a lot more than I used to. I wonder where civilisation is taking us. They haven't found a cure for cancer, but they're trying to put men on the moon. I used to worry about the bomb. Oh yes, I went around under a cloud of doom. But I live by the Bible and I read in it that we should not worry about such things; that death comes when and where it wishes, and we must have faith and wait.'

During the Easter school holidays after the pantomime ended, he joined some teachers from his old school, Cheshunt Secondary Modern, who were involved in the Crusaders' movement, on a boat on the Norfolk Broads. 'I thought it would be a bit of a drag,' he admitted afterwards to *The Daily Mirror*. 'But it was marvellous. They asked me to bring my guitar and we had sing-songs aboard in the evenings. If we went ashore they called me Harry, but a few people holidaying on the Broads did recognise me. When we got to a place called Reedham there were some girl fans waiting.' On the boat, Cliff helped with the washing up, the cooking, and getting in supplies – and told me that there were regular prayers and daily readings from the Bible.

To the London *Evening News*, he said he still drew only £10 a week pocket money: 'And I often don't spend all that. People think I must be a millionaire. I'm not. Nowhere near it. I have to ask my accountant if I can afford it before making a big purchase. At present I'm hoping to get his consent to having my tennis court repaired . . . my mother cannot get over that we have three cars. Nor can I. I keep asking myself why so much should be paid to me. It's impossible to accept it calmly. I'm always asking myself "Why?"' To the music paper *Disc* he said: 'Records don't mean all that much any more . . . sometimes I'd love to have a job where I could work regular office hours and have weekends off.' To the *Daily Express* he said: 'I attend Crusader Bible classes for youth in Finchley. Boys and girls go there to hear talks on the lines that a Christian's life can be fun. I sort of jolly them along. I'm also president of the Members Council of the National Association of Youth Clubs. I now arrange my work to have weekends free for youth activities. All my closest friends are teachers. We take parties of young people for holidays on the Norfolk Broads – messing around cooking over camp fires, to Whipsnade Zoo . . . I'm catching up with the things I missed myself as a teenager. I feel I could do a lot more with my life. If this feeling continues for another year I will make a decision about my future. I could probably work in show business for the next twenty years. But if the day comes when I don't feel satisfied, I'll get out . . . if I give up show business I would like to teach drama or religious education. I'd soon find out during my two years in training college whether I had an aptitude or not. This week I gave an off-the-cuff talk on "Tolerance" at a school speech day – Ingatestone Secondary Modern, where my former history teacher is now head master. I managed all right.'

Talking to the *Evening Standard* of his involvement with the Crusaders, Cliff said: 'It's a kind of a way of life. It's a moral way of life. I've always tried to be a bit moral, a bit Christian and not ashamed of it.' Saying that two of his sisters had now become Jehovah's Witnesses, he said: 'I can't tell you the change it has made in their lives; the confidence is ridiculous.' He recalled that he had come into show business at the age of seventeen 'and when you come in you lose your childhood immediately. I find all this specially fun because I never did the youthful things.' He admitted that he was beginning to feel dissatisfied with his work. 'I don't get the same kick out of my life that I used to . . . I feel I could do more with my life.'

Clearly his whole direction was changing – in his work as much as in his thinking; it was announced that on January 31st, 1966, he would open with The Shadows in cabaret at the Talk of the Town in London, the first time a group had ever been engaged to appear at what was recognised as the West End's top night spot.

While he was appearing there I interviewed him back stage one evening just before he was due to go on with The Shadows, and the answers he gave indicate just how deep the changes were that he was undergoing; he was now very different from the Cliff Richard I had first seen performing seven years earlier:

QUESTION: YOU HAVE JUST MADE YOUR LONDON CABARET DEBUT. WILL YOU NOW BE CONCENTRATING ON CLUB APPEARANCES?

ANSWER: Not particularly. I had always wanted to play at the Talk of the Town. This was really achieving an ambition.

QUESTION: DO YOU PLAN ANY MORE THEATRE TOURS?

ANSWER: There are none planned at the moment because of this film. We were due to start 'Aladdin' five months ago but there have been troubles over the script. We just can't get it right. (That was the film version of his Palladium pantomime.)

QUESTION: WHAT SORT OF DIFFICULTY HAVE YOU HAD?

ANSWER: I saw the script and approved the outline. But we couldn't get it right after that. We have had four writers working on it, three of them American. I don't care who writes it. I'm just waiting for someone to have a date for me to start filming. I told them nine months ago that I wanted it all to be over by August 1st.

QUESTION: WHY PICK THAT DATE?

ANSWER: My holidays.

QUESTION: BUT WHY DO YOU HAVE TO TAKE YOUR HOLIDAYS ON A PARTICULAR DATE?

ANSWER: Because I am taking two car loads of friends down to my house in Albufeira. They are all school teachers and we can only go in the school holidays.

QUESTION: TONY MEEHAN WAS REPORTED TO HAVE HELPED YOU PLAN YOUR CABARET ACT. DID HE?

ANSWER: He works for us now, full-time. He helped us make our last two or three records, and our next one 'Blue Turns To Grey'. Mick Jagger and Keith Richard of the Rolling Stones wrote it for us and we recorded it about a month ago.

QUESTION: IN WHAT LANGUAGES DO YOU NOW RECORD?

ANSWER: French, German, Spanish and Italian.

QUESTION: CAN YOU SPEAK ANY OTHER LANGUAGES FLUENTLY?

ANSWER: No. I tried to learn Portuguese between shows while I was in pantomime last year. A tutor came in to help me with it, but it was pointless trying, with so much going on. I would like to learn French because that would carry me through most countries.

QUESTION: ARE THERE ANY COUNTRIES YOU HAVE VISITED THAT YOU WOULD NOT LIKE TO GO BACK TO?

ANSWER: No. Luckily we have been very successful in all the countries we have played overseas, so we would like to go back.

QUESTION: ARE THERE ANY COUNTRIES THAT YOU HAVE NOT BEEN TO THAT YOU WOULD LIKE TO VISIT?

ANSWER: Yes – Japan. I don't know why particularly; it's just things I have read about Japan. I would like to see the place for myself.

QUESTION: WHAT SORT OF SOCIAL LIFE DO YOU HAVE NOW?

ANSWER: It has nothing to do with show business. None of my friends are in show business. I never go to parties – well that's not quite true. I went to one on Monday for the first time in two years. It was at Muriel Young's house. Dave Clark, Cilla Black and Cathy McGowan were there. We spent two hours discussing religion.

QUESTION: BUT YOU NEVER GO TO NIGHT CLUBS?

ANSWER: I suppose I ought to go to these discotheques since I am supposed to be a pop star. But they just don't interest me. What's this one? The Scotch of St James, or something – even The Shadows go there now, but not me.

QUESTION: WHERE DO YOU GO THEN?

ANSWER: Tonight I went swimming at my old school in Cheshunt.

QUESTION: WHY DO YOU GO BACK THERE SO OFTEN?

ANSWER: I still keep in touch with my old English teacher, Jay Norris. She's always taken an interest in me and in my career. If I hadn't gone into show business she would probably have guided me into something else. Now the other teachers at the school are close friends, too. Some of them are my age – Bill Latham and Graham Disbury. They weren't even at school when I was there. They will be going down to Portugal with me in the summer.

QUESTION: HOW OFTEN DO YOU GO BACK TO THE SCHOOL?

ANSWER: I will be there again tomorrow. My club, The Vale in Finchley, has got up a badminton team. We are playing the teachers.

QUESTION: ARE THERE ANY OTHER SPORTS YOU PLAY?

ANSWER: Tennis. I had a tennis court built at the back of my house last summer. I often have friends round to play.

QUESTION: DO YOU WIN?

ANSWER: No. Not at tennis, but I'm not too bad at badminton. I suppose I shouldn't say it but in fact I'm quite good.

QUESTION: HAVE YOU ANY BUSINESS INTERESTS OUTSIDE SHOW BUSINESS?

ANSWER: I have a film company, Inter State, and two music publishing companies, Joaneline and Eugene Music. But I haven't really diversified. I'm not a very good businessman. I don't go round looking for songs for my company like a good song publisher should.

QUESTION: HAVE YOU EVER THOUGHT OF ENDING YOUR CAREER AS AN ARTISTE AND BECOMING AN AGENT LIKE YOUR AGENT LESLIE GRADE?

ANSWER: No – but I could leave show business tomorrow. It wouldn't bother me one bit. I'm sure of that. I know now that if someone was to tell me that I couldn't sing any more it wouldn't worry me at all.

QUESTION: WHY IS THAT?

ANSWER: It's just the way in which I've changed. If someone had told me that four years ago I would probably have hanged myself (laughing). But I have changed a lot.

QUESTION: WHEN DID THIS HAPPEN?

ANSWER: It was about two years ago. We were on tour and I just wasn't getting any satisfaction out of my work. After each show I just went to bed. Then I started thinking about other things outside show business.

QUESTION: IT HAS BEEN SAID THAT YOU WOULD LIKE TO BECOME A TEACHER. IS THIS SO?

ANSWER: I would. Quite honestly, I would love it. I like working with young people. When I first joined the Young Crusaders at Finchley it was a bit difficult. They thought of me as Cliff Richard, but after a few weeks they got used to me, and I can go down there now and be treated like any old Joe Dokes. It would be the same if I became a teacher.

QUESTION: WHAT SUBJECTS WOULD YOU LIKE TO TEACH?

ANSWER: Divinity and English.

QUESTION: WHAT AGE GROUP?

ANSWER: From 11–15. It would have to be a secondary modern school. My friends who are teachers tell me it is easier teaching children who find learning easy, but much harder teaching those who find it difficult. In any case I think young children at primary schools should have women teachers.

QUESTION: WOULD YOU TEACH BOYS OR GIRLS?

ANSWER: Mixed, I think.

QUESTION: LAST NOVEMBER YOU SPOKE AT INGATESTONE SECONDARY MODERN SCHOOL SPEECH DAY ON TOLERANCE. DID YOU FIND THIS UNNERVING?

ANSWER: I was scared stiff. This was something completely new to me, but I loved it. Since then I have also spoken at a boys' school in Lewes, Sussex, where one of my friends teaches. Then I spoke for 35 minutes.

QUESTION: HAVE YOU TAUGHT AT ALL YOURSELF?

ANSWER: Well, yes – in a funny sort of way. Jay Norris told me that instead of recording all those pop songs I should record some poetry. She wanted to show her children that poetry was beautiful. So I went around to her house with a tape recorder and we recorded twelve poems, which she now uses in her English lessons. That gave me a bigger kick than winning a Gold Disc.

QUESTION: YOUR LIFE NOW THEN HAS LITTLE RELATION TO SHOW BUSINESS?

ANSWER: Not socially. The morals in this business are much worse than anywhere else. You can go to the village where I live, Nazeing, and find people there living good lives but not in show business. It's funny really because you don't get bakers or chartered accountants behaving like some people do. Immorality has no excuse. It is no good to say that show business has special temptations.

Life is full of that and there is nothing really so special about show business.

QUESTION: WHY DO YOU THINK PEOPLE HAVE THIS VIEW?

ANSWER: It is the attitudes people have. Take John Lennon. In one interview John was asked what he thought of my voice. He said he thought I sounded Christian, and he meant that as abuse. Now that doesn't worry me. After all he has that image. But what does concern me is his frame of mind. He uses the word 'Christian' as though it were a form of weakness, when in fact it is a strength. Some of the strongest men in history have been Christians.

QUESTION: DID LENNON'S COMMENTS UPSET YOU?

ANSWER: No, they didn't upset me. But I wonder if he behaves like that when he goes home to his wife. Is he sarcastic to his family? Someone who is genuinely sarcastic is like that all the time and not just in interviews.

QUESTION: TWO OF YOUR SISTERS HAVE BECOME JEHOVAH'S WITNESSES. HAVE YOU?

ANSWER: No, but I did come very near to it. They have had a great influence on my thinking, but I can't parcel up my views into any neat formula. I just know I'm a Christian and that's as far as I can define it.

QUESTION: HOW DID THIS START?

ANSWER: While I was on tour about two years ago. Licorice Locking was with us then and he is a Jehovah's Witness. He is now full time with them. I still see him sometimes.

QUESTION: NOWADAYS YOU ARE SELDOM SEEN PLAYING THE GUITAR. DO YOU IN FACT STILL PLAY?

ANSWER: Only privately. I play a lot at youth clubs and take my guitar with me when we go away camping. Last Easter we hired three boats on the Norfolk Broads, seven of us in each boat, and we had a sing-song each night.

QUESTION: YOU HAVE SAID YOU MAY STILL BE BACKED BY THE SHADOWS WHEN YOU ARE

35. DO YOU IN FACT WANT TO SPEND ANOTHER 10 YEARS ON THE STAGE?

ANSWER: Why not? If I was no longer happy I would give it up tomorrow. After all we have done everything now. We would be embarrassing if we went on singing 'On The Beach' when we were 35, but in fact our act is changing all the time. In cabaret we sing Frank Sinatra ballads, and if tastes change then so will we.

QUESTION: YOU DON'T THINK YOU WILL GIVE UP SHOW BUSINESS JUST YET THEN?

ANSWER: How can you say. I might give it up next year – or in ten years' time. I just don't know. As a child it was my ambition to be a singer and I came into show business very young. I was only 17 when we had our first hit. I still enjoy working in show business but if ever I ceased to do so I would give it up immediately. And I would have no regrets.

That interview, read again nearly ten years later, reveals I think just how much consideration Cliff Richard had been giving to his work as an entertainer, and how his whole thinking had changed since he first came into the music business; I have interviewed him many times since then – and in my view he has changed comparatively little. That period appears to have been the great turning point in his life.

The change became suddenly very apparent the following June. That was when he chose to make public the depths of his religious convictions.

In those early months of 1966, it was quite evident that his career was in any case already moving into a new phase; that season at the Talk of the Town, for instance, brought him before an audience that was even wider in range than those he had played to before – even though it was a famous London cabaret spot, noted for its cabaret and dining facilities, one night twenty-seven teenagers from Norfolk hired a coach to travel down there to see him. And the four-week season was so successful that he and The Shadows were booked to appear for an extra two weeks. 'The people who wouldn't necessarily come to see me at a theatre rock show and yet put themselves out to watch us on TV are the type who are coming here now,' he told the weekly paper *Music Echo*.

It was quite clear too that he had made a special effort to appeal to this wider audience from some comments he made on the planning of the cabaret act to the *New Musical Express*: 'We decided that it would be wrong to attempt something drastically different – after all, I don't consider myself as a Buddy Greco. So we shall stick largely to the type of material which is expected from me. But I shall be introducing a couple of new numbers into my act. I've come across an old Frank Sinatra number which I like immensely, called 'My One and Only Love', and we're also going to put that in. And I shall also be doing 'My Colouring Book', which I have recorded, but which I have only performed live on one occasion – and that was on television . . . (The Shadows) will be the basic core of the act. But when the house orchestra is needed – such as for the opening routine and ballad accompaniments – it will be used.'

Soon after the Talk of the Town season, it was reported in one of the music papers, *Disc*, that he had now definitely decided to leave the music business – but this was counter-acted by the news that he was to make another film 'Finders Keepers', for which The Shadows were writing the music; that he had TV appearances planned, and was already planning to open in the pantomime 'Cinderella' at the London Palladium the following Christmas.

But then on June 16th, 1966, he joined Billy Graham on stage at his Crusade meeting at Earls Court, and publicly announced his commitment to Christ. That morning *The Daily Mirror reported*:

> Those teenaged fans who have been mobbing Cliff Richard over the years are in for a surprise tonight.
>
> If they turn out to hear him sing, their screaming voices will almost certainly be stilled in awe at their pop idol.
>
> For Cliff, minus the twanging of beat guitars, will sing a simple gospel song, 'It's No Secret', for the Billy Graham crusade at Earls Court, London.
>
> It will be his testimony of why he believes in God.
>
> Last night Cliff talked about his decision to join the Billy

Early Cliff

Shadows, Cliff and birthday cake '74

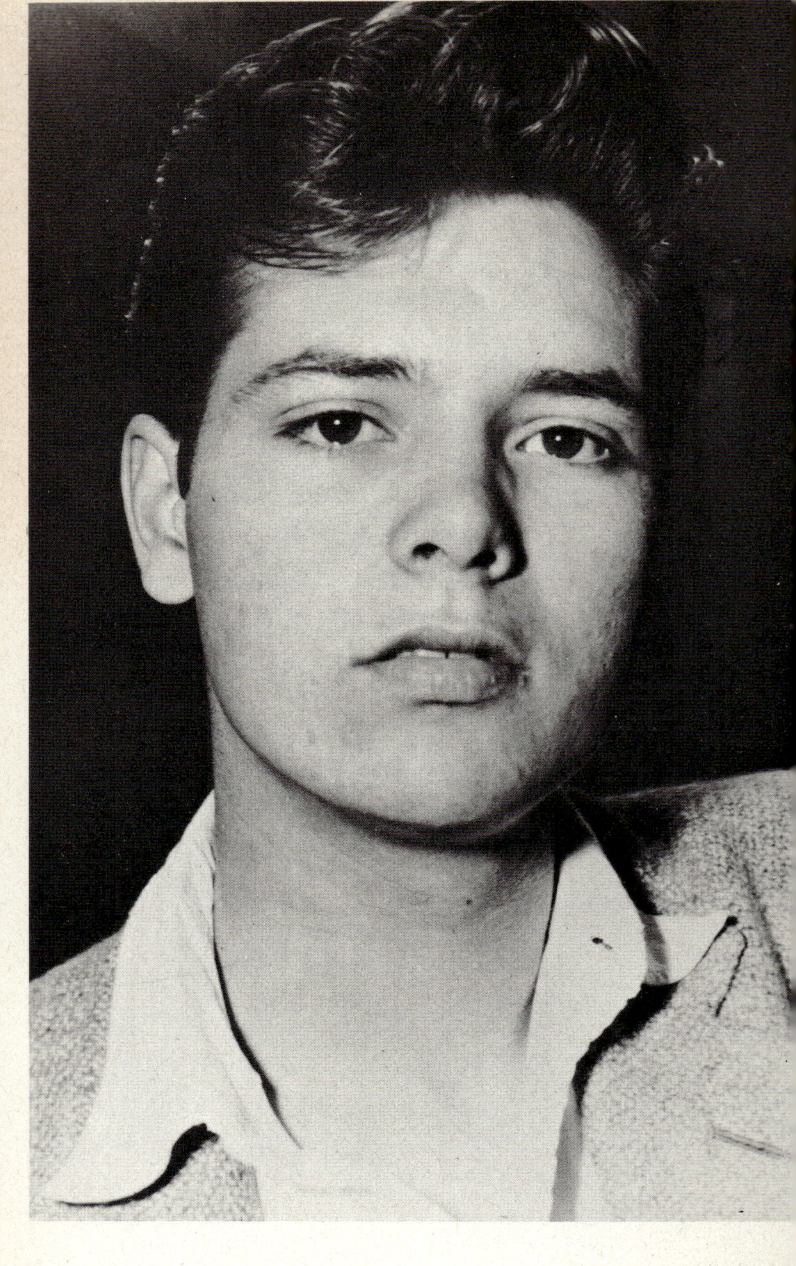

Cliff with two showgirls

Top Of The Pops '73

Cliff on the 300th Top Of The Pops

The Shadows photographed on The Lulu Show on Sunday 13th Jan '75

Cliff Richard photographed during rehearsals for The Royal Command Performance

Cliff and Hank

Cliff

Cliff and Olivia Newton-John

Graham set – a decision that could paint him 'soft' in the eyes of the beat fans.

'Anyone who thinks a Christian is soft can think again,' he said.

'It took me a long, long time to pluck up enough courage to tell the world "I'm a Christian".

'But when I did I knew I had scored. Now I can make something out of my life.'

Will his Earls Court appearance tonight be an attempt to 'convert' his fans?

'No,' said Cliff. 'That's not the reason I'm doing it. I just felt this was a wonderful opportunity for any Christian.

'In fact, I shan't be Cliff Richard at all, really I shall just give my testimony as any other Christian would do.'

That night there was an audience estimated at 25,000 at Earls Court when he walked up to the stage, wearing a velvet jacket and his horn-rimmed spectacles – and then afterwards he went outside and spoke to another crowd, estimated at 5,000, who were unable to get seats inside the building.

In his first speech, he said. 'I was fortunate that in my childhood my mother and father always had the Bible at home. I can only say to people who are not Christians that until you have taken the step of asking Christ into your life, your life is not worthwhile. It works. It works for me . . . I have never had an opportunity to speak to an audience like this before. Young people often ask "Is Christianity relevant to our way of life?" It definitely is.'

Afterwards, Billy Graham told *The Daily Express*: 'I think this has a tremendous impact on young people who have listened to Cliff or seen his films. For him to stand up and say "I am a Christian" gets thousands of young people thinking.' And later Cliff himself commented: 'I've never been so scared as I was before going up on stage. We didn't have a rehearsal or anything like that.' And asked whether he would now be giving up show business, he said: 'I don't want to be in show business all my life. But I have commitments for some years yet. When I do give up I won't wear a dog collar, but the idea of becoming a religious instructor appeals to me . . .'

Within forty-eight hours there was another Cliff Richard sensation that also made the front page of many national newspapers. His mother, Mrs Dorothy Webb, now aged 45, married again – and the man she married was Cliff's own former chauffeur, Derek Bodkin, who was 24 and younger than Cliff himself. This, too, was to totally change Cliff Richard's way of life.

CHAPTER SIX

While the whole emphasis of Cliff Richard's career was changing, and while he himself was becoming so much more committed to religious work even to the point of planning at one stage to give up show business altogether, The Shadows, too, were beginning to move in a different direction; they had become stars in their own right, firstly through recording independently from Cliff and following that world-wide hit 'Apache' with a run of hit singles between 1960 and 1965 and then later through their separate concert tours, stage shows and TV appearances.

Inevitably, it was Hank Marvin and Bruce Welch who attracted the most attention; they had been associated with Cliff Richard since 1958 and with the departure of first Tony Meehan and then later Jet Harris they became more and more the pillars of the act both musically with their songwriting and also in terms of presentation. Other members of the group seemed to go their separate ways without affecting the popularity of The Shadows.

Although only their bass guitarist for eighteen months, Licorice Locking was to have a lasting effect on both Cliff and The Shadows themselves; it was largely through his influence that Hank Marvin became a Jehovah's Witness and that Cliff himself began to devote so much of his time to religion. To this day he remains a close friend of them all even though it is now twelve years since he left, and has always been ready to step in and help them out when they needed him – when they appeared at the Talk of the Town for a season in cabaret without Cliff in January, 1968, his successor John Rostill was unable to play for the first part of the booking after having a nervous breakdown and that was one occasion when Locking temporarily rejoined the group. (That booking was fraught; their drummer Brian Bennett was also taken ill and had to go into hospital with appendicitis – which brought Tony Meehan back into The Shadows briefly and Cliff himself also sat in on drums as well.)

Locking had formerly played with the Vagabonds skiffle group and had backed Terry Dene (who also left music to devote his time to religion) and Marty Wilde, and before joining The Shadows had accompanied Adam Faith, Joe Brown, Brenda Lee, Eddie Cochran, Gene Vincent and Conway Twitty. His last work with The Shadows was an appearance with Cliff Richard on ATV's 'Sunday Night At The London Palladium' on November 3rd, 1963, and recording the music for 'Wonderful Life' (though he did not travel to the Canary Islands with them to take part in the film itself). When he left, manager Peter Gormley told the *New Musical Express*: 'We are sorry to lose Lick. He has been a big asset to The Shadows, but he's asked to leave and there's nothing we can do about it. We wish him every success in the future.' And Cliff himself told the *New Musical Express* that he admired Locking for taking the decision, though he was sad they would no longer be working together.

Locking told the *New Musical Express*: 'I feel I must have more time to myself, to devote to the things I feel I must do. I love being with The Shadows, but the constant touring does not allow me to fulfill my promise to life . . . I have thought about this for a long time. It has become a strain to divide myself in two – being loyal to The Shadows and travelling with them, and being loyal to my belief, for which I feel I must stay in one place and do good work there.'

Until Locking's announcement, Bruce Welch – who had often been troubled by ill health – had been thinking quite seriously of leaving. Indeed, his departure had been announced a month earlier in *The New Musical Express*, which reported that a Harley Street specialist had advised him to take a complete rest and to cease touring when he had sought the specialist's advice after missing several performances during the Blackpool summer season show. 'It is terribly unfortunate – the last thing in the world I want to do,' Welch said. 'But if the doctor says it's the best thing, I have to listen to him.' Cliff Richard was quoted as saying: 'It's going to be a terrible wrench for all of us, after five years of close harmony. But you can't argue with your health.' And Hank Marvin had said: 'Bruce has a wonderful rhythmic sense and distinctive style, and we're going to miss him very much as an integral part of the group, quite apart from our personal feelings.' It was said that Welch would, however, continue to be closely associated with Cliff Richard and The Shadows running the group's record company, Shadrich, and their music publishing companies, probably working with Tony Meehan who was expected to produce records for the company.

But with Locking's decision to leave, Welch changed his mind, saying that he had rested during their tour of Israel, was planning to spend three weeks in Barbados with his wife, and then expected to join the group for the filming of 'Wonderful Life' in the Canary Islands, where he thought he would also be able to catch some relaxation. 'I'm feeling much better,' he said. 'Our next assignment is in March, by which time I should be right as rain again . . .'

Although John Rostill, who replaced Locking, and the drummer Brian Bennett, who had taken Tony Meehan's place, were to be associated with The Shadows for many years, it was now Marvin and Welch who largely led The Shadows; when Welch went temporarily into management and music publishing they continued to be closely associated, and then after The Shadows had broken (the dates for all this are given in the chronology in the appendix) they came back together again to form the trio Marvin, Welch and Farrar

John Farrar, a talented writer and arranger as well as guitarist, had first met the group in Australia when he was with one of the top Australian groups, The Strangers, who played one concert together with The Shadows in Melbourne. 'I stood in the wings that night and heard John play – and he was good,' Bruce Welch later told me. But that was not the only thing that brought them together; by another strange coincidence John Farrar married Pat Carroll, a singer who had been in a double act with Olivia Newton-John, who was to later fall in love with Bruce Welch. In fact they lived together for some time planning to marry, but then the romance ended.

Olivia, born in England but brought up in Australia and the daughter of the Master and Vice Chancellor of two Australian universities (Ormond College in Melbourne and Newcastle University in Sydney), told me of her part in bringing John Farrar into the group. 'Pat (Carroll) and I originally came to England after winning a talent contest in the Johnny O'Keefe

TV series in Australia, but we stopped working together and Pat returned to Australia to marry John while I stayed on in London, where some of my family were still living . . . I always kept in touch with Pat. We used to write to each other regularly, and I'd known John as well. When Hank and Bruce told me they were looking for a third member of the trio they were forming, I told them about John, and he sent them over some tapes. I told them he was a top guitarist in Australia, and also had a strong falsetto voice . . . and Hank and Bruce asked him to come over from Australia to join them without any audition, and before they had really met – apart from that one time that Bruce had seen him play.'

Although he had mailed over those tapes, John Farrar himself had no idea what was going on until he received a phone call in Melbourne from Welch, who was calling from London and woke him up in the early hours of the morning. 'I knew something was afoot, but I had no idea what it was,' John later told me, 'because Bruce had tried to phone me earlier and had left a message at my mother's house. I had been out working, and had gone home with my wife and we were both fast asleep around 1.30 am when the phone rang. When I picked up the phone and Bruce told me what he was planning, I couldn't believe it. Pat wanted me to drop everything and fly to London on the next plane, but I was desperately trying to be cool. That year (1970) had been such a good year for me already – I had been out to Vietnam entertaining American and Australian troops there, and I had been to America for the first time studying recording techniques at studios on the West Coast, and I'd been on honeymoon to Hawaii. Suddenly, my life seemed to be changing in all directions and then on top of all that came this phone call asking me to drop everything and fly to London.

'Pat and I didn't go back to bed until the following morning. We spent the whole night smoking cigarettes, drinking cups of coffee and talking . . . I was trying so hard to be cool, but if the truth be known I wanted to get on the next plane, too.'

In the end, it was not as hurried as that. Hank and Bruce agreed to give Farrar three months in which to settle all his commitments in Melbourne; to give The Strangers reasonable time to find a replacement for him, and for him and Pat to dispose of their flat and furniture. 'My group were very good about it – they were sorry I was going, but glad for me,' said Farrar.

By the time Marvin, Welch and Farrar came into being, two years had passed since The Shadows had broken up; apart from looking after their publishing interests and helping to launch The Virgil Brothers, Welch had spent much of that time relaxing. 'For ten years The Shadows had been my whole life,' he told me. 'I had never done any other kind of work, and had come into show business straight from school. Suddenly, it was all over – and when I woke up the next morning I thought, "Gosh. What have I done!"

'I decided to take a complete break. I have a house in Portugal, and spent many holidays there. Olivia and I also made three trips to the United States, and we spent some time in the country riding horses and playing tennis. Apart from some work in the office, I spent those years doing absolutely nothing – but I missed working which was why Hank and I decided that we would form a new group, though completely different in style from The Shadows. In the past we had always played electric guitars; now we decided to go acoustic . . . the challenge is to persuade people to like the new kind of music we are creating.'

Meanwhile, Hank Marvin had stayed in the working side of the business, continuing with the solo work that he had started even while The Shadows had still been together. In many people's minds, he had become the leader of the group – because he still kept on working, seemingly as strong as an ox, even when Bruce Welch had periods of illness; when Brian Bennett and John Rostill had been ill in turn. And when Cliff Richard had announced his planned retirement from show business, Hank had made it plain that he would still carry on working. 'I'm glad he's made a decision over his retirement because he'll obviously feel better for having done so,' Marvin told *Disc and Music Echo*. 'It's his personal choice, but I feel he will be a big loss to the entertainment world. But it is his personal happiness that should come first and this is what he wants to do. I don't think his retirement will have a bad effect on The Shadows. We've done an awful lot of work on our own in the past few years. Our concerts and cabaret work have always got good results, so I don't see that losing Cliff will have a harmful effect on us. In any case we'll be trying all the harder now, because we won't have Cliff to hide behind any more.'

That same year (1967) Hank and The Shadows had made an eight-week world tour, visiting Spain, Turkey, Israel, Japan, Hong Kong and Australia, and then afterwards appearing with great success at the Yugoslav Song Festival.

In Australia, one of their bookings was in cabaret at Chequers, the top night club in Sydney – and the comments from the local critics show how firmly established they had become as a separate act from Cliff Richard. In the *Sydney Daily Mirror*, Sydney Mann wrote: 'Because of a very heavy schedule I had to forego their opening show a week ago and did not not see them till Thursday. While the audience, which comprised the young, and plenty of the not so young, clapped and clapped, I observed four young men sartorially elegant in the style of pseudo Regency Bucks wearing boots fashioned from delustred satin no less. Casey was right, they WERE killin' em. These four youngsters are also, if you will permit another literary lapse, colossal, stupendous, fantastic, wonderful and absolutely great. I have heard many an opening night audience call for more but I've never heard an audience mean it like they did at this show. These fellows as far as I am concerned are not The Shadows, they are the substance.'

In the *Sydney Sun* Norman Kessell wrote: 'Ever wondered how a live top mod group would sound if you could remove that blanket of squeals from the Stadium? A rare chance to find out occurs this week and next at, of all places, Chequers. And from one of the very best groups in the business, too – The Shadows. This most unusual Chequers booking is bringing off the year's biggest night-club gamble. And although I have seldom seen so many young people in a night club, it is the oldies who led the applause – many of them perhaps discovering here just how good and exciting this music can be.' Another Australian show business writer David Frith commented: 'How The Shadows have changed since Australia last saw them accompanying Cliff Richard on a wild tour in the pre-pop Beatles era . . . then they were a quartet of weedy youngsters, playing pulsating rock 'n' roll to a shrieking teenage audience. Now they're back – four smooth, well-dressed, mature young men, playing to predominantly middle-aged audiences at Sydney's Chequers night spot and drawing a standing, cheering ovation.'

In the *Sydney Sunday Telegraph*, Allan Barnes wrote: 'We were sitting watching the most unlikely act Mr Dennis Wong, Chequers' owner, has ever put into the place – the English pop group The Shadows. I know that Mr Wong had grave misgivings about booking such a group, but on opening night on Friday to his – and my – astonishment the place was packed; other anxious patrons were queuing up the stairs in Goulburn Street and running the phones hot with bookings. These four lads are brimful of personality, pleasant of manner and voice and – if you dig the Top 40 sound – are apparently accomplished musicians of their type. One's foot taps almost involuntarily to their beat.'

In those days Hank Marvin and his first wife Beryl with their four children, Dean, twins Peter and Paul and the youngest Philippa divided their time between a home in London and a country cottage in Norfolk. In one interview Marvin told me that having been brought up in the country he thought he 'probably couldn't stand it for long' if he had to live in the country all the time. 'But it's nice for the kids to have fresh air, and if they're brought up in natural surroundings I think they have a greater regard and appreciation of nature; they learn not to abuse it. I think it's character-building, and a lot more fun for them than a town . . . I get great pleasure in trying to enjoy life. I enjoy things you might think are stupid . . . when I'm driving through a particularly beautiful place in the country, I feel a sort of joy in being alive. It might seem stupid to people who are looking for happiness in something else . . . I enjoy working on the land around the cottage. There's a great therapeutic effect in digging earth until your hands are covered with callouses, or in attacking eight foot high grass with a scythe because it's too long for a motor mower. You feel tired afterwards – but it's a wholesome kind of tiredness.' Admitting then that he was a stern father and believed strongly in discipline, Marvin referred to his own schooldays in Newcastle-upon-Tyne – and said that he always had the greatest respect for those masters who caned him the hardest. 'I thought twice about playing them up the next time,' he said. 'I was caned very hard once – it hurt for three weeks. A certain amount of physical punishment is necessary for a child – and sometimes for criminal delinquents.

'We were playing in the Isle of Man once and a policeman told us about some lads of about twenty-three years old who had been drinking, and were walking along the road swearing loudly. A man asked them not to swear in front of his wife – so they beat him up. They got a birching, and the policeman said they were crying like babies – and admitted it was the greatest humiliation they had ever experienced in their lives. That wouldn't happen in England – but I bet they didn't beat anyone up again!'

When he first married, Marvin had kept the fact secret. It had been in 1960 when most people in the music business believed it could be fatal to their careers to admit they had a permanent relationship with just one girl because fans would be jealous. 'It seems so silly now, but everyone kept their marriages quiet in those days,' Marvin told me. 'When I first met The Beatles, John Lennon wouldn't even tell us he was married – he introduced Cynthia to me as his girlfriend. In those days, everyone in this business was afraid of losing fans if it became known they were married. Look what happened to Marty Wilde; he disappeared. But fans are very different nowadays. They realise that even pop stars are human – and, in fact, our own fans are very faithful. We're lucky we have a very broad appeal – not like the Pink Floyd, who are too errie, or The Rolling Stones who generate musical excitement, a sort of musical sex. We're playing very simple music, which is easy on the ear. And we try to keep up a good standard. We're not trying to set the world alight.'

In 1968, Hank and his first wife separated; later they were divorced and he married Carol Naylor, a dancer and former wife of Terence Edmund, who played PC Sweet in the BBC TV series 'Z Cars', and in 1971 he and Carol made their main home in Devon, buying a seventeenth century mansion at Higher Wiscombe near Southleigh, Honiton. The house is surrounded by 53 acres of parkland, and is approached along a half-mile long private drive. 'We have moved here for peace and quiet,' he told the local paper *The Western Times*. 'I have wanted to live in the country for a long time and I hope to have a go at farming.'

Later he told me that the house was built around a quadrangle, with one of the barns supposed to be the remains of an earlier, probably Saxon dwelling house. 'It's in a beautiful valley with wild deer, and not a pylon in sight,' he said. 'My next door neighbour moved down there two years ago, and Carol and I have kept in touch with him. Then we were staying down there with him, and we fell in love with the countryside. The people there are real country people, with a quieter pace in life which I like very much . . . the first thing I noticed when we moved in was the quiet. At night, I would lie in bed and all I could hear was the hooting of the owls. Then during the day I'd look out of the window and see wild deer – roe deer and fallow – wandering about the shrub across the field from the house. Sometimes in the morning when we're having breakfast, rabbits come scampering across the lawn right under our window . . . I've stopped the fox hunters coming across my land. They came across my land twice without my permission, and now I've told them they cannot cross the land again. I'm not against all forms of hunting. It's reasonable enough for a man to go hunting for food. I can understand the arguments for thinning out deer, killing the weakest so that the strongest deer continue the breeding line . . . but I can't understand fox hunting, these people dressing up for the day, and killing for fun as a social sport. I don't accept that at all, and all this "blooding". I suppose if I mixed in their social circle, I would be ostracised for not letting them hunt on my land . . . but the friends I have are not in that sort of fraternity.'

The only times Marvin leaves Devon now are to work with The Shadows or with Cliff Richard; before the group reformed he appeared in two BBC TV series with Cliff, and continued writing and recording – his compositions have included songs like 'The Day I Met Marie', 'Throw Down A Line', his own single 'London's Not Too Far' (released in 1968); many of the songs for the films 'The Young Ones', 'Summer Holiday', 'Wonderful Life' and 'Finders Keepers', and others which he has written with other people like 'Nivram' (co-written with Jet Harris), and three, 'Midnight', 'That's The Way It Goes' and 'Why Can't It Be Me' with Bruce Welch as well as the music for that pantomime 'Aladdin', which he and Welch also co-wrote. Their partnership is one of the most successful – and most under-publicised – in British music.

'The titles takes us longer to think of than actually writing the songs,' Bruce Welch told me. 'Honestly, the songs themselves don't take all that long – but sometimes we have to wait weeks before we find the right title, something out of the ordinary, but not too banal.' But he thinks the wait is worth it when they come up with originals like 'Genie With The Light Brown Lamp', 'Stars Fell on Stockton' and 'Rhythm and Greens', which are all puns in their way. ' "Rhythm and Greens" was just a play on rhythm 'n' blues,' explained Marvin.

'The songs with lyrics are simpler than the instrumentals,' Marvin told me. 'We just take an easy phrase like "I met a girl" – I wrote a song with that title in just thirty minutes one evening, playing around with a tape recorder. The idea for the lyric and the melody came almost together, and I just pressed on from there . . . the instrumentals take much harder work. "The Rise and Fall of Flingle Bunt" was one of our accidents. We were just playing around at a recording session and the tune just came up – and we got the name from two actors who had appeared in several films with us. Melvyn Hayes and Richard O'Sullivan. Whenever they forgot lines at rehearsals, they would fill in by mumbling, making up things about characters they invented. One of them was Flingle Bunt.

'When I wrote that song "London's Not Too Far", I had this idea of this young girl watching her hero on TV and leaving home to see him – it happens, doesn't it? – and wrote the words and music in half-an-hour. It all came very quickly. Next morning I went over it again to see what changes I wanted to make, but I was quite satisfied with it as it was.

'It's difficult to explain how we start writing a song. I mean, there is no set formula. We don't have to be in any particular mood – just productive. We start strumming on guitars or messing about on the piano and suddenly someone will come up with a set of chords or a melody line . . . if we are contracted to write numbers, we just have to sit down and write them, anywhere, anytime.'

For someone who has probably had a wider influence on British pop music than anyone other than The Beatles in that his guitar work encouraged so many of today's top musicians to take up the instrument, Marvin has surprisingly broad tastes. He told the *New Musical Express* that Josh White, Big Bill Broonzy and Leadbelly had been his own early influences when he was switching from skiffle to rock 'n' roll. 'These people like Clapton have always been heavily rooted in the blues and the feel of the music. It was all new to me, so it would have been difficult to play that stuff well. I'm quite convinced that you have to get into the feel which is quite different from rock 'n' roll . . . there are a lot of good ones (guitarists) around. Like Eric Clapton is marvellous. He did a lot for that style of guitar playing and I admire what he did. Also I like a lot of the stuff Leslie West's played with Mountain and some of Jeff Beck's stuff is good as well. Then there's people like Paul Simon, classical players like Segovia, flamenco players like Paco Pena, and I also like some of the early stuff from Chet Atkins . . . I enjoy playing guitar but I suppose I'm not that dedicated. I don't think you can have a family and all that and be as one hundred per cent dedicated as you were when you were 17 and might play day and night. For me, too many years have gone by and too many things have happened for me to be completely dedicated to the instrument.'

When I asked Marvin which song or piece of music that he had heard during his life as a musician had made the most impact on him, he replied rather surprisingly: 'I think the most lovely piece I have heard is Rodriguez' "Guitar Concerto". I have a version by Narcisso Yepes, but Segovia has also recorded it. I'm also very fond of Tchaikovsky's 4th Symphony, which Brian Bennett first played to me years ago – and I went out that day and bought it. That is still one of my favourite pieces.' When I commented that I had been expecting him to name a more contemporary number than that, Marvin said: 'Oh, there's lots of those – "Bye Bye Love", "Wake Up Little Susie", "That'll Be The Day" and "Peggy Sue". They all bring back a great deal of nostalgia for me, as do some of the early Presley records like "Mystery Train" . . .'

Like so many of today's successful musicians, Marvin has used the fortune he has made from pop music to carve himself a very different lifestyle from that traditionally expected of stars in the entertainment business; he has that ancient house with its large park in Devon, a large library of books and an extensive record collection; having spent so much of his life playing once and often twice-nightly he now practices relatively rarely, and it is only quite recently that it has dawned upon him that The Shadows really have been one of the major guiding forces in British pop music in the past two decades.

Now he says he would like to write a novel, and also a collection of children's stories because he has always enjoyed being surrounded by young children, and seeing their faces as he invents romantic and surrealistic tales. 'They keep telling me I ought to write them all down,' he says.

Perhaps he will one day, and then maybe people will realise that he has long been a much under-estimated man.

CHAPTER SEVEN

When Cliff Richard's mother Mrs Dorothy Webb decided to marry again, the wedding seemed to come as big a surprise to Cliff as it did to the national press; the *Daily Mirror* reported that the wedding 'was such a well-kept secret that not even Cliff was told until *AFTER* the registry-office ceremony . . . Mrs Webb telephoned Cliff, 25, from a call-box after the wedding at Epping, Essex, and broke the news.'

For the press it was quite a story – for the man she married, Derek Bodkin, was only twenty-four years old (younger than Cliff), and had been Cliff's former chauffeur.

After the wedding, the couple returned to the family home at Nazeing. The champagne bottles were opened, and out on the lawn Cliff himself started taking the wedding photos with just two of his sisters, Jackie and Joan, there with them. And then Mr and Mrs Bodkin drove off for a touring honeymoon travelling in Cliff's own white E-type Jaguar.

'I'm not worried by the difference in their ages. Derek is an old friend,' Cliff told the *Daily Mirror*. 'Mum has told me that the reason she kept it all a secret was that she didn't want it to be a showbiz wedding with lots of people there. She wanted to be married quietly and this was the only way she could do it. She wanted to be just plain Mrs Webb getting married, not Cliff Richard's Mum.'

Later a large party of journalists went down to Pinewood Studios where he and The Shadows were working on their fourth major film together 'Finders Keepers', in which the female lead was taken by the actress Viviane Ventura, and there Cliff found himself at the centre of a press conference on the film set – now very much the figure-in-the-news with his public alliance with Billy Graham at Earls Court, and then his mother's remarriage happening so soon afterwards. He explained that since starting work on the film he had been staying with a friend in North London so as to be nearer the studios – and but for that he would probably have been at the wedding. 'It's her life,' he said. 'I hope she and Derek – I can't call him

Dad – will be very happy. I'll be buying them a house as a wedding present and they'll be going to my place in Portugal for a honeymoon. I'll also buy a house for my sisters if they want one, and one for my aunt and teenage cousins, who have been living with us. Then I'll sell the big house I have and probably get a flat . . . I didn't know (about the wedding) until Saturday morning when they phoned me. I bought some wine and arrived for the celebrations after the ceremony.' He said he had known Derek Bodkin for many years; that he had worked for a car hire firm at one time that he had often booked and had later become his personal chauffeur, and was now working as an undertaker's assistant in the East End. 'He hasn't worked for us since my father died – we all regard him as a friend,' said Cliff.

Asked about his decision to make that public announcement at the Earls Court crusade meeting, he said that he was a member of the Church of England and attended a church in Finchley, adding: 'I did a Billy Graham study course for about five weeks and found it stimulating, and then I received a letter asking me to appear at the meeting and said I would . . . Billy Graham is a wonderful man, absolutely sincere. He couldn't speak night after night the way he does if he weren't.'

While the film was still in production, he went straight ahead and sold his home at Nazeing, 'Rookswood', to a London businessman for £43,500 – and then bought his mother a house in Broxbourne, Hertfordshire, and another two houses nearby for his two sisters and his Aunt.

Cliff himself continued sharing a house in North London with his schoolteacher friend Bill Latham and Latham's mother, and later they bought another house together which continues to be his home to this day. 'I hate living on my own,' Cliff explained to the *Daily Telegraph* when he was interviewed there. 'I tried it once and it didn't work. I like home cooking and people to talk to.'

After all the house-moves had been arranged, I talked to him again and among other questions asked him what was the most extravagant thing he had ever done. 'Buying that house at Nazeing,' he said surprisingly. 'It was only extravagant to the extent that I didn't realise at the time that my sisters would move and my mother would get married again, and that I'd be left there on my own. I sold it again – for a bit more than I paid for it, but we'd had a lot done to it so I came out about equal. I don't miss it. You don't miss extravagant things because they're unnecessary.'

Whenever one met Cliff Richard in the years thereafter, one could see that he had found himself; that the years of doubt had gone. He was much more self-confident – sometimes wearing glasses, sometimes not (for personal appearances now he nearly always wore contact lenses); his hair style had changed considerably, combed forward, and much longer than it had ever been before – and his clothes were now well-cut, contemporary-styled, often bought at the most exclusive shops in Bond Street. 'My friends think I'm going hippie,' he said one day, with a disarming smile. 'I like to try something different now and again. I'm just getting a bit cheeky, though my clothes are not usually over bright. Some of these groups really overdo it. You see them all dressed up, and they look as if they're in fancy dress – the sort of clothes I buy I would be proud to wear anywhere . . . I read this journalist somewhere who said I was now buying clothes in Carnaby Street. Not me! Nothing but Savile Row and Bond Street,' he said, smiling again, now prepared to be much more self-deprecating than he had ever been before.

While his religious work was becoming ever more widely publicised, Cliff Richard's show business career also seemed to be moving into a different gear; quite clearly he had found for himself that very same self-confidence he had noticed in his sisters.

'I've never been so happy in my life,' he told me one day with considerable emphasis. Talking about that Earls Court crusade meeting, he said: 'I suppose quite a lot of people thought it was a publicity stunt, which of course it was – but not for me, for Billy Graham.' He was now thinking quite seriously of becoming a teacher and even changing his name so as to make the break more final; he told me that besides Licorice Locking and Bill Latham, another very important influence in his life had been the actress Susan Hampshire, with whom he had worked on the 'Wonderful Life' film. 'At that time I had no strong ties with the Church, but Susan had – and later she went out to Lambarene to work with Albert Schweitzer,' he told me. 'While we were sitting around the film set waiting to work on different scenes, we talked a lot together. I owe a lot to her. She helped me to come closer to the Church.'

When I asked if there were any other people who had influenced him, he said: 'There are a number of people I admire. I'd like to be a combination of Billy Graham and Albert Schweitzer, because they both have this calling. Schweitzer was a brilliant musician but he could go and live in squalor, helping the lepers, and he was dedicated. Billy Graham had so much knowledge as well as belief. He seems to know so much about things like politics and is able to equate all that with his beliefs. I don't have that kind of talent. I can't express myself so well.'

Although he was still saying that he might leave show business, Cliff Richard was soon finding that he could combine both sides of his life – and when he had some religious work that he wanted to do (which was usually crusade meetings, speeches to schools, visits to churches, etc, for which he would be given many months' advance notice) he would simply phone up Peter Gormley's office and give them warning that he would not be available for any show business offers that came in for the dates in question.

'I get lots of requests to do church work,' he told the London *Evening News*. 'I feel it is my duty to do it. If it really came to a choice, I would hinder my career rather than stop . . . I have always believed in God and always prayed, but that doesn't make me a Christian. Being a Christian, to me, has been a step I didn't realise I had to take . . . I know now I could live on £20 a week if I wanted to.'

In October, 1966, he shared a platform at the Royal Albert Hall in London with the Archbishop of York, Dr Coggan, and the Bishop of Coventry, Dr Bardsley, and a group of evangelical singers at celebrations to mark the 21st anniversary of the Lee Abbey evangelical training centre. Cliff Richard told the audience: 'As a Christian I feel it is my duty to take every opportunity to profess I am a Christian and that I personally was saved by Jesus Christ. It is so easy to make the initial step. It is what follows that is not so easy . . . I'm still terrified to appear on a platform.' He then sang two Gospel songs. That same month he was taken to lunch at the Athenaeum Club by Canon Frederic Hood, Canon Residentiary and Chancellor of

St Paul's Cathedral. 'I have never met him before. A friend suggested we might have lunch,' said Canon Hood. And when it was suggested that this was probably the first time a pop singer had stepped inside the door of the Athenaeum, Canon Hood replied: 'That is rather why I asked him.'

In the November it was reported that Cliff Richard was to be confirmed as a member of the Church of England, which he duly was by the Bishop of Willesden, taking his first Communion at his home church in Finchley. And then it was announced that he would be making a film specially for Billy Graham's organisation, 'Two A Penny', for which he would be writing the songs himself and appearing as Jamie Hopkins, who falls in love and finds that his relationship with the girl (played by Ann Holloway) changes as she becomes aware of Christianity. In the early days of their relationship he had been an atheistic drug peddler, but through the romance Hopkins finds a deeper meaning to life.

The film was produced to a budget of £150,000 by the same production crew that had recently been involved in the films 'Alfie' and 'Khartoum'; the cast included such well-established actors and actresses as Dora Bryan, who played Hopkins' mother; Avril Angers, who portrayed his landlady and had recently finished the John Mills–Hayley Mills film 'The Family Way' and Geoffrey Bayldon, who had been in the films 'To Sir, With Love' and 'Casino Royale'. And then in one scene Billy Graham himself was shown, filmed at that Earls Court crusade meeting. A press release for the film gives some idea of the way the Billy Graham organisation saw Cliff's involvement:

> 'After a decade as Britain's top pop singing star, Cliff Richard now tackles a new, dramatic role – for the first time audiences will see him acting tough, dynamic and dangerous in "Two A Penny", a World Wide Films' production in Eastmancolour.
>
> 'Contemporary and outspoken, it is the story of today's ruthless youth – fighting their elders right now in every country – seeking, not necessarily in that order, money, power, love and truth. But where lies Truth for such as the young man portrayed by Richard in "Two A Penny" – selling kicks and getting them the hard way, in a society of de-

valued ideals and shattered destinies?

'"Two A Penny" is a picture with a point of view, which also turns over the other side of the coin, in a forthright manner which will not only surprise Cliff Richard's multitude of fans, but also the many who believe – or disbelieve – that there is a better world than the one we see around us today.

'It is, in fact, significant that an entertaining film in our time can face such challenging issues and make of them a motion picture for which the top distributors are keenly bidding for their home and overseas markets.

'Co-starring in "Two A Penny" are Dora Bryan and Avril Angers, while the picture introduces to the screen charming newcomer Ann Holloway (a cousin of Stanley Holloway), as the troubled girl so desperately and romantically involved with the young anti-hero. Actuality is the keynote of this unique production, shot on the streets of London and on various recognizable and also new locations north and south of the Thames – not least of which is a special screen appearance by the evangelist Billy Graham, whose work in action in the integral drama of this film is shown with questing reality, in such a manner as to give every member of the audience a truly remarkable view of the threat confronting all humanity today: Alter, or Perish . . .'

While the film was still in production down in the Goldhawk Studios, just behind Shepherds Bush Market, I interviewed Cliff Richard there in his dressing room when he told me that the actors' trade union Equity had insisted that he must be paid the minimum weekly actors' wage of £40. 'I wanted to do it for nothing, but they told me I had to take £40 a week – and I have to accept the money – so I shall be giving that away to charity, probably to the film company itself. They need the money,' he said.

'I realise that I'm laying myself open to criticism from some people in making this film. There are even a few swear words in the script – a couple of "bloodies" – and there are two fight scenes. I even *lose* one of the fights,' he said laughing at the improbability of such a thing happening in any of the other films he had made. 'But essentially this is a love story about a

1967 type of relationship. When the film starts off, neither the boy nor the girl believe in anything . . . he is a person without any real morality, willing to do anything to make money. You can see that their relationship has been pretty free with him demanding sex at any moment, and then the film shows how their relationship changes as she becomes more aware of Christianity . . . but when the film ends, the boy has still not been converted – and I think that is one of the strengths of the plot. You are left wondering what will happen to him.'

After making that film, he continued to take on bookings and religious engagements that covered a much wider area, often visiting churches in different parts of the country to talk to young people in the congregation, often playing a few songs on his guitar, and often coming out with surprisingly controversial statements of the kind that one would never expect from a show business star.

For instance, when he spoke to a congregation at Cuffley in Hertfordshire Cliff Richard said: 'People who just sleep around make the most unhappy marriages. The divorce cases are mostly made up of people who have had sex before marriage . . . pre-marital sex is unhealthy to the mind.'

When it was suggested by a reporter from *The Sunday Times* that with his wispy fringe of hair and slender body he looked like a young Mia Farrow, Cliff Richard replied: 'I've lived for years with people saying I'm a poof but I don't give a damn. My best friends know me and that's all that matters. Even before I became a Christian I wasn't going to lay loads of chicks to prove myself . . . I'm about the only one around who hasn't had a nervous breakdown . . . of course, I'd like to marry. I was near about three years ago. I went to my manager and said what happens with the marriage bit and the fans? We agreed it was worth losing ten per cent for the marriage. I never got round to asking the girl, though . . .' And when asked about Billy Graham, he said that 'as a bloke (he) doesn't bother me a bit. In our film we've cut him down to four minutes . . . as long as he doesn't preach them, he can have any political views he wants. Fortunately, he just preaches about sin and morals.'

He also released an album 'About That Man', which was largely devoted to readings from the New Testament with four religious songs. 'I was shattered and amazed when people criticised it,' he told the *Melody Maker*. 'That they should dare to talk like that about the New Testament. They seemed to see it principally as a musical album, and it was not intended as that. The idea was that it should be used in schools as a work only for very young people. It would be nice if it did influence people in the direction of Christianity, but I don't think a record such as this can . . .'

And then he appeared in another film for Billy Graham, a documentary on the Holy Land for which he re-visited Israel, and those towns and villages mentioned in the Gospels. He joined the inquiry into pornography set up by Lord Longford together with the Archbishop of York (Dr Coggan), Lord Justice Edmund Davies, Lord Soper, Lord Shawcross and Malcolm Muggeridge; appeared at a convention for the Methodist Association of Youth Clubs, performing to an audience of 6,500 at the Royal Albert Hall, London; joined Billy Graham on stage at Wembley Stadium in 1973 when the evangelist returned for another crusade (this time sharing the platform with American folk singer Johnny Cash). He made two television series for the Northern-based company Tyne Tees TV, singing gospel songs with The Settlers; also appeared with The Settlers at religious charity concerts in different parts of Europe. He took part in a religious crusade to Japan – and was awarded the National Viewers and Listeners' Award 'for his outstanding contribution to religious broadcasting and light entertainment' after which Mrs Mary Whitehouse commented that he was 'very forthright about his Christian faith but at the same time this makes him in no way priggish. In my view he is precisely the type of young Christian one wants to see.'

These were just some of the major events – quite apart from all that he continued to regularly support his own church in Finchley, and to spend some days most months visiting churches and affiliated youth organisations in different parts of the country.

As all this progressed, it became more and more evident that he was very happily combining his interest in religion with his show business career. 'I should never have said I was leaving the business,' he told me. 'It was a big mistake. Ever since then the Press have been trying to get me to name a date – and I no longer have a date in mind . . . until quite recently I never believed that it would be possible to combine all my other interests with a show business career, but now I am finding I can, though I've never said that I am *not* leaving show business. If it ever reached the stage where I had to choose one or the other, I have no doubt which one I would choose. I could never have done that 10-week world tour with The Shadows, for instance – I would have missed my Bible studies for ten whole weeks if I had done that, and I just couldn't do that.'

When one spoke to him then, he was never afraid to speak his mind even if it meant criticising other artistes. He would tell you which records he thoroughly disliked; would talk about people he had met through his religious work, quite naturally and without affectation – and sometimes would come out with a turn of phrase that would seem almost unlikely. When George Harrison was very much in the news with his own particular religious views and his album 'All Things Must Pass', Cliff Richard told me mid-conversation: 'And if you see George Harrison, you can tell him I think he's a load of old rope!'

He told me how he tried to fit in both sides of his life into a crowded schedule: 'If I get a letter in the morning post asking me to talk to some school, I just ring up the office and ask if that day is free. If it is, I ask them to keep it free – if not, I just say I'm sorry that I can't manage that particular date. But I never try to fit in things like that when I'm filming. Unless I'm working on a film, when I really have to give my whole time to it, I can usually manage a talk or something like that as long as I am given about two months' notice. We've always worked on the principle that we never try to do two things at once, and that's how I'm trying to combine show business with all these other interests. I just think of them all as different aspects of my life, which have to be fitted into a schedule like anything else. But until it actually happened to me, I just never imagined that it would be possible to organise myself like this . . . what I want to do is continue recording and grow up as an actor. I've discovered that I don't have to give up show business and teach scripture to be a Christian.'

Indeed, it is probably true to say that he was fast discovering that it was his continuing success in show business that was enabling him to be so effective in his religious work. In the years since 1966 his career has followed a remarkably even pattern, with one hit record following another and with a succession of major achievements as an entertainer.

His first achievement was that fourth film with The Shadows, 'Finders Keepers'. The idea for that film had come from George Brown, who had produced 'Guns of Batasi' and had just finished 'The Trap' with Rita Tushingham and Oliver Reed. 'During the hectic search for the missing American bomb off the coast of Southern Spain this year (1966) I thought there was scope for a film,' said Brown. 'The same time Leslie Grade mentioned to me they were still short of a story for a Cliff Richard film. Well, for five days and nights I sat down and wrote a story while the Spanish-American bomb affair was still current.'

The film, which also featured Robert Morley, Peggy Mount, Graham Stark and John le Mesurier as well as Viviane Ventura was in production for nine weeks at Pinewood, and at that time Cliff was still sorting out his affairs after his mother's marriage and his decision to sell what had been their home. 'Material assets and wealth just don't interest me any more,' he told me on the film set. 'I know now that I can do without all that . . . I'm in no hurry to move into another house. I'm quite happy where I am. They like having me here, and I like being here. If we've got nothing to do then we go for long walks in the country, or watch television in the evenings – I like "The Man From Uncle" and "Star Trek". I don't worry about anything now like I used to. If I want to go down to the shops, then I do – and if someone recognises me then I quietly draw them into a shop doorway so as not to get a crowd gathering around me, sign an autograph, and go on my way. Once or twice a week I pop down to the record shop in Waltham Cross – the one I always used to go to when I was a kid – and that's where I buy all my own records.'

This remained his private lifestyle as the film finished and he attended its premiere as well as that of the puppet film 'Thunderbirds Are Go', for which he and The Shadows were seen as puppets themselves performing the soundtrack music, and then he and The Shadows began another long session at the London Palladium, this time appearing in the pantomime 'Cinderella' with Cliff as Buttons. The following summer while The

Shadows were making their world tour he appeared in that semi-religious film 'Two A Penny' for the Billy Graham organisation; visited Japan in the October, and then began work on a Christmas television pantomime 'Aladdin' for Rediffusion TV – as it was announced that he would be representing Britain in the 1968 Eurovision Song Contest, which was due to be staged at the Royal Albert Hall on April 6th, with the BBC televising it to seventeen different countries and also behind the Iron Curtain.

'I wanted the best to represent Britain and in Cliff Richard we have the very best,' said the then head of BBC TV Light Entertainment, Tom Sloan. Cliff Richard himself later admitted in an interview with *Disc and Music Echo*: 'If I'd been asked a couple of years ago to compete for Britain in the Eurovision Song Contest, I'd have turned the invitation down flat because I would have been afraid to lose. And that isn't being patriotic. It's purely because I wouldn't want to have risked damaging my reputation by failing to be first . . . today things like that don't matter to me any more. I'm content to coast along but I'm past the point of worrying over my career. Look, my records seem to climb to about Number Six in the charts and no higher. Well, that suits me. I don't have any great ambition to be Number One any more . . .'

But the song that was chosen for him by 170,000 BBC TV viewers who sent in entry forms when he sang a short-listed six for them to choose from did just that – 'Congratulations', written by Bill Martin and Phil Coulter, took him back to Number One in the music paper charts for the first time in three years, though he only managed to come second in the contest itself. To make sure that it was a hit around the world Cliff recorded thirty different versions of the song in various languages.

Although they still worked together, his career now often seemed to be quite independent of that of The Shadows. Just as he was preparing for Eurovision, Cliff also made his debut in a TV play playing a fortune-hunting thief in 'A Matter of Diamonds' (ATV). 'This is a perfect opportunity to add a completely new and fascinating direction to my career, but this doesn't mean I shall be giving up any other part of my work,' he said. And then he appeared at the Talk of The Town without The Shadows – though they came back together again to record an album and to appear in a Rediffusion TV special to mark their tenth year in the music business.

As that anniversary approached, he was asked by *Disc and Music Echo* whether he thought he had made any monumental mistakes. 'Honestly no,' said Cliff Richard. 'If I had made a monumental mistake at any stage of my career, it would have left a scar on my career and I don't have a scar. We quelled "Cliff-mania" and it became a standard following. There's been no one disaster. Admittedly, a couple of times people have had a go at me – at the "Wonderful Life" film and the recent TV play "A Matter of Diamonds" . . .' Asked how he had reacted to all the anti-Cliff Richard quotes from The Beatles, he replied: 'I just found it all rather pointless when I read or heard about their remarks, because it didn't make them rise in the public's eyes. They felt they had to say clever things in front of the press, but when John Lennon, for example, came out with that quote about The Beatles being more popular than Jesus Christ, I regarded it as the height of childishness for a supposed adult cynic . . .'

His friend Hank Marvin told the same paper: 'We don't socialise so much these days, mainly because the Shads have been away working abroad and in the provinces, while Cliff does an awful lot of stuff for the evangelistic movement. So we're both leading very full lives . . . he's much more mature, of course, but he appears to be just as ambitious as he was then. Perhaps more so. He has an aptitude for being able to concentrate on whatever he does and succeeding. He's giving more and more of his time to helping others through his Crusader work, and this is a change in him – taking time off when he could be earning money to work for something that brings him no cash return. He was a young, enthusiastic lad and this he hasn't lost. He'd rave about some clothes he'd seen, or a song, a film, or a girl, and it's still exactly the same. But then he was unaware. Now he is aware of what he is and what his position entails . . .'

After those charity gospel concerts in Europe – in Zagreb, Stockholm and Amsterdam with The Settlers, Cliff Richard and The Shadows came back together yet again for a twelve and a half week variety season at the London Palladium in the autumn of 1968, and then The Shadows went their separate ways while Cliff spent 1969 and 1970 continuing his career at the level he had now established it, taking part in religious meetings in many different parts of the country, releasing a new single approximately every three months just as he had always done, working on that film on Israel for Billy Graham, appeared on television shows to promote his records, and occasionally appeared in concert (all the dates are given in the appendix).

'Nothing new ever happens to me,' he told me one afternoon. 'I'm a fairly happy character. I don't have great moods of depression. I get frustrated about things occasionally – when I go to schools and the kids ask questions, and you can see that some of them are just being cynical. What right have young people of that age to be cynical? They're wasting their time. I'm as contented as anybody can be. You never can be really contented, though – you don't have any right to be. I don't want to be a millionaire, but before I took up Christianity my accountant arranged a pension scheme for me so that when I am sixty I can retire on a fantastic pension. It won't be all *that* fantastic, but it's a form of security. I would like to go on working until I am sixty if I can . . . I believe in tithing. After all I give ten per cent to my manager and to my agent, so why not to God? But you can't arrange it as easily as that, so what we've arranged is that ten per cent of my work is arranged so that all the money goes into a trust fund for charities.'

At that time he frequently had long holidays; drove an expensive car, a Jensen (justifying it by saying that it was important that he travelled comfortably so as to arrive fresh for each engagement), and still kept up his tennis, basket ball and some badminton.

'I don't want anybody to think I am anything but what I am,' he told me. 'I don't intend to become a conformist Christian, though I'd be careful about drinking in public and about the films I appear in – though I wouldn't mind playing an immoral character in a film if the film made a positive point.'

In 1970, he also accomplished another ambition – making his straight acting debut in a stage play at Bromley New Theatre as the young son in 'Five Finger Exercise', returning there again the following year to appear in Graham Greene's

'The Potting Shed'. 'I was so bucked when I did "Five Finger Exercise" because I had to develop a particular walk for that part, and it must have been convincing because my sister asked me whether I'd hurt my leg,' he said.

By then he had regular TV series for the BBC, often running to thirteen weeks and appearing with Una Stubbs and Hank Marvin. He was again making annual concert tours in Britain – and even spent six months touring Europe, Israel and the Far East in 1972 before making another seven-week tour of Britain, accompanied on both itineraries by Olivia Newton-John. 'We weren't scheduled to have any time off at all,' Olivia told me. 'But the concerts in Singapore and Korea were cancelled because the authorities there thought Cliff's hair was far too long, which made us all laugh . . . we got caught in a typhoon in Ngoya. After two shows, we were due to catch a train, but then they told us we couldn't because this typhoon was coming. We were at the top of a restaurant building and could feel it swaying. Looking out of the window we could see roof-tops being blown down the streets. The electricity went off three times. I was in a panic, but then it went absolutely still. Apparently at that moment we were right in the middle of it. When we were finally able to leave, we found no trains were able to run so we had to travel 100 miles by taxi to the next town; the journey took us four hours, driving through several floods and we heard later that four people had been killed in the typhoon . . . on our days off we went to see the palaces and a few Buddhist temples. I loved the custom of taking your shoes off before going into the temples . . . they were beautiful, with so much gold work . . . and we also saw a couple of Kendo exhibitions, with people learning to fight using wooden poles instead of swords . . . when we left Tokyo, which is very westernised, I felt we were beginning to see more of the real Japan. Kyoto was set against mountains which made a perfect background for all the greenery surrounding the palaces . . . one evening Cliff and I and three other people went to see "The Creatures The World Forgot" with Julie Ege, which was pretty abysmal. Another night we saw Cat Stevens do a show in Tokyo. He was in the same hotel as us so we all had dinner together . . . other times we ate in Japanese restaurants, sitting on floor cushions, though they do provide back rests for Westerners – the food is cooked in front of you on hotplates and you take it straight off the hot plate while you're having the meal.'

Early in 1973, Cliff Richard returned yet again to the Talk of the Town in London for another three weeks in cabaret. He appeared on 'The Cilla Black Show' on BBC-1, again singing songs from which was to be chosen the British entry for the 1973 Eurovision Song Contest, in which he sang the British entry 'Power To All Our Friends' – becoming the first person to be chosen twice to represent Britain in this annual contest. The song itself earned him another Gold Disc for world sales, though it only reached Number Four in the British music paper charts – and immediately after the concert contest he left for another overseas Gospel Concert Tour, this time to Australia and New Zealand. He also made another film 'Take Me High', in which The Shadows were not involved at all; the music was all written by Tony Cole with roles taken in the movie by George Cole, Debbie Watling and Hugh Griffith.

Now he was frequently taking two holidays a year – plus another two weeks at Easter to continue his annual boating jaunt on the Norfolk Boards with the Crusaders. The pace had slackened down in his show business career, though he was still combining this with his religious commitments, choosing the work carefully with his manager Peter Gormley. In the autumn of 1974, he released his first album specially recorded as a studio project in four years – 'The 31st of February Street', including for the first time four of his own songs. He appeared with the re-formed Shadows at a Palladium concert to raise funds for the widow of the BBC TV producer Colin Charman, and then began an almost leisurely tour of Britain, with the dates well paced so that he could take it all in his stride. Nevertheless he still worked hard: one of the most remarkable qualities Cliff Richard possesses is that he seems to have a talent for using every day – even if the work he does is not necessarily for money.

'I've no idea how much money I earn,' he has told me not once, but several times, and I think it's probably true that he has far less actual wealth than most people believe because he has now spent much of the past ten years working for nothing, and yet still giving ten per cent of all he actually does earn to charity.

'I've played concerts and never known whether they've made a profit or a loss,' he told *Disc and Music Echo*. 'I really don't work for the money, yet of course I could never do the work for nothing. People can say, "If money doesn't mean much to you, why do you charge for concert appearances?" But I have to. It's like the man who handed out £5 notes on street corners. People wouldn't take them because they suspected there was a fiddle. They'd think the same if I started appearing for peanuts! I agree, though, that it's only when you have money that you realise how little it means . . . if I thought my money could convert anyone to my beliefs, then I would give it away. But money doesn't change anything. John Lennon could never be converted because of my money . . . (but) no-one needs vast sums of money. My father raised our whole family on £11 a week, and we managed. I'm positive I could live very happily on £30 a week.'

CHAPTER EIGHT

Cliff Richard remains a curious figure in today's music business; he is still a best-selling artiste in most countries outside the United States and as a performer of Gospel songs and therefore in effect an evangelist he has either sung or lectured in many European cities, in South Africa, Australia, New Zealand and Japan as well as nearly every major centre in Britain – and yet the business which he came to dominate with The Shadows between 1958 and 1963 is now a world-wide industry that has moved on without him.

Although much of today's most popular music is either recorded in Britain or composed abroad by musicians and songwriters who have grown up in this country, the greatest fortunes are being made in the United States which forms well over half the world's record market – and that is one area where Cliff Richard has never risen to the top, even though he was the first British pop star to tour the United States, and has frequently recorded there and appeared on the major US television shows. And then there is the fact that he has written very little original music himself, though Hank Marvin and Bruce Welch are two of the most successful though still under-recognised composers of the past fifteen years.

In fact, measured by the standards of today's rock music industry, Cliff Richard's creative achievements have been remarkably few; and yet he is a major star – make no mistake of that. In Britain he and The Shadows are almost the only performers who have successfully crossed the barriers from pop music into the world of the all round family entertainers – the world of Christmas pantomimes, Palladium season shows, the TV special, the Eurovision Song Contest, the provincial concert tour with stage orchestra, or the film-musical-for-all-the-family. And they have remained at that level, entertaining not only successive generations of teenagers but also their parents and their younger brothers and sisters, since making that big switch in 1960. There are very few other artistes in the world who have stayed at the top for fifteen years.

Still unmarried and still very boyish in appearance, slim as a stripling youth, and espousing religious causes with a fervour that no-one else has in British show business, Cliff Richard has in fact become a symbol of youth – as the Churches have seemed quick to recognise. Which tempts the questions: Can he really be as single minded as that? Is he sincere? Has he no vices? Can one person really be as 'nice' as Cliff Richard appears to be?

The answer to all these questions is 'yes'. Cliff Richard is almost the same person now as he was when he started; religion was always a strong influence in his home in childhood, and now he is merely giving public expression to what have long been his private beliefs. Although he is very ambitious, and is well known within the music business for being very conscientious in rehearsals and in preparations for personal appearances, he is also quite self-effacing – though he admits to a personal vanity which expresses itself in the care he takes in buying clothes, in looking after his appearance, and in dieting.

There was one occasion when I met him that he was wearing a jacket made of buffalo hide trimmed with Japanese fox fur, over black velvet trousers, with a pastel green and pink flowery shirt open at the neck, with a chiffon scarf knotted loosely, the whole outfit accentuated by what was obviously a very expensive pair of gold rimmed glasses. 'I've actually got a pair of trousers to match the jacket,' he told me, 'but the first time I wore them they gave me a rash so I haven't put them on again since. I expect the hide probably wasn't treated too well . . . I just fell in love with this suit. It was one of those extravagant moments when I didn't ask the price. I just wandered into Cordoba in Bond Street, which specialises in these exotic clothes and tried this one, and by the time they had it pinned for the alterations and I asked what the price was, I thought I had gone too far to change my mind . . .'

That hardly sounds like the Cliff Richard of the Earls Court crusade – but this is all part of the enigma. Since discovering that he could successfully combine his show business career with a very active schedule of religious commitments, Cliff Richard has seemed to become more relaxed in every way; he dresses more casually, expresses himself more freely, and seems far less afraid of causing offence than he was in the days when every well-trained pop star had to be non-committal on nearly every subject when meeting the press.

Fire a question at Cliff Richard now, and he comes back with an answer which may not be what you expect from a leading artiste – but which is his own opinion nonetheless. For instance, I asked him whether he thought young people should have the vote at eighteen and he said: 'No – I don't think anyone knows enough about it to vote at that age. At eighteen, you have only just finished your GCE's and maybe you have worked for a year – but that's not long enough to know how to vote. In fact, I've never known which way to vote. I mean, I do care what happens but then I start to think, "Well, what difference is my little vote going to make one way or the other?" Of course, I know that if everyone thought like that nothing would ever get done – but my talents don't lie in politics. Anyway, I think people vote for the wrong reasons; not for what is best for the country, but for emotional reasons or inherited ones. "My Dad voted Conservative, so I'm going to vote Labour because they're going to make everyone equal" – you know what I mean?'

Ask him now for his impressions of life in South Africa, and Cliff Richard is no longer cautious before replying. 'It's pretty troubled out there,' he told me after his South African lecture tour in which he accompanied the Reverend David McInnes, Precentor of Birmingham Cathedral, and sang his Gospel songs at rallies in the major cities. 'The people are all so insensitive. I came back from South Africa more confused than I had ever felt about any other situation in my life. I've been there three times now, and I still can't fathom it out. The prejudice runs so deep. It's not just black people and white people – the Asians don't like the negroes, the Chinese don't like the whites, and there's this racial hatred running through every section of the community.' He said that he had come face to face with this just once, and that was when he was staying in a Durban hotel and was told that an Indian photographer wanted to take some photographs of him. 'I invited him up to my hotel room, and when I saw the people's faces in the hotel I thought for a moment that they were going to arrest me – but they had more sense than to make a martyr of me. I really did hope that they would throw me into prison for breaking the racial laws and asking a coloured man into a white hotel because that might have brought it home to people. But they are too clever out there to make a mistake like that. I know that if I was married with a wife and a family, I wouldn't want them to go and live in South Africa.'

In many ways, his views are conservative – he says he finds the concept of the permissive society 'ludicrous'; that he regards anarchists as 'unrealistic', and he told me one day that he was wholly in favour of film censorship. He went even further than that in an interview with *Melody Maker*. After swipes at David Bowie ('I really dig his music, but his campness kills it for me') and at Alice Cooper ('. . . to me Cooper is totally unhealthy. He is fake philosophy, when he tells his audience to get rid of their inhibitions. How does he help them when they see him chopping up a doll and hanging himself? I really don't know why he does it.'), Cliff Richard went on to talk about Andy Warhol: 'I haven't seen any of his films, but as far as I'm concerned they stink of titilation. I saw a film recently about a child rapist – "The Offence". It was violent and showed a man being beaten to death, but it was far more valid because it made an impression. I can still remember the scenes vividly. As far as I can see it's better to learn about sex from parents or by personal experience. Mary Whitehouse and Norris McWhirter had every right to stop that film (referring to Warhol). Mrs Whitehouse is ten years ahead of her time.' After commenting that he thought the cinema medium was being wasted and that he supported censorship, Cliff Richard was asked if he would be willing to appear in a film with a bedroom scene and replied: 'I would never take my clothes off. I can't see how it's necessary to go into detail over such matters. I saw "Romeo and Juliet" – that had a bedroom scene, but it was done in such taste that there was nothing wrong. The nearest I've ever got to that kind of thing was in a film I made for Billy Graham called "Two A Penny". In that there was some dialogue of that nature and some fumbling, but nothing more. Often I think I'd like to see some pornography, but in my saner moments I know I don't need to. I don't want to be turned on by anything except by the person I love . .'

It is easy to mock Cliff Richard, and many people in the music business do. His views are unfashionable and to many people's minds out of date – but he is aware; he is not a prude; he is not priggish, and he does practise what he preaches.

His home is still that modern house in North London that he shares with Bill Latham (who arranges many of the engagements in his religious diary for him) and with Latham's mother, who looks after the house for them. He still sees a great deal of his family, who still help him choose every record that he releases; he is generous both to them and to his personal friends, and genuinely enjoys occasions like Christmas when all his closest friends join together for the midnight service on Christmas Eve, and then meet again on Boxing Day to distribute presents in what is 'always a very noisy day, because all our friends and families are there . . . that's when we give out the presents. I like to buy presents for everyone like food hampers for the girls who work in the office, toys and games – always something fairly attractive.'

By the standards that generally prevail in the world of entertainment, his life-style is simple. Unless he is visiting another congregation he always attends his own Church every Sunday; attends the Crusader classes every week if he can; takes those annual boating holidays every Easter on the Norfolk Broads; usually manages a game of tennis, squash or badminton at least once a week or goes swimming in summer; eats very simply so as not to put on weight (he gains weight very easily and so diets cautiously); watches television nearly every night when he is not working. Most weeks he pops down to the record shop in Waltham Cross that he has known all his life and listens to the new LPs and singles that have come in, usually buying five or six records at a time ('I like to know what I'm buying,' he says). He drives himself everywhere, not bothering these days to have a chauffeur; he still has occasional back trouble, though since being healed by prayer he no longer has to wear the steel corset that he once wore daily and he no longer has to take pain-killing tablets. At least once or twice a year most years he slips away to his villa in Portugal, often accompanied by a few friends (at other times of the year the villa is available to members of his family and other close friends who wish to go there).

'I make no secret of the fact that I am using my career to promote Christianity,' he says, at the same time criticising those who put pop stars on a pedestal. ('They don't deserve it," he says. 'They don't have any more to offer the world than other people.')

'I must admit that I sometimes look through my diary and see how far ahead everything has to be planned, and I get that feeling of being snowed under. There are moments when I feel that I would like to live in a tiny country cottage, miles away from anywhere, with no phone . . . but then I couldn't do that, could I? Look at all the things I would have to give up.'

CLIFF RICHARD CHRONOLOGY

This chronology, the most detailed record so far published of Cliff Richard's career, is compiled from the files that the author has kept since 1961. In the early years Cliff and The Shadows made very frequent British tours. The dates for those and for their many appearances on long-forgotten TV shows have been omitted – but the important moments in his career are all here: —

1939

6 July. Terence Harris ('Jet' Harris) born in Kingsbury, Middlesex.

1940

9 February. Brian Bennett born in London.

14 October. Harry Roger Webb (Cliff Richard) born in Lucknow, India.

1941

28 October. Hank Brian Marvin born in Newcastle.

2 November. Bruce Welch born in Bognor Regis.

1942

16 June. John Rostill born in Birmingham.

1943

2 March. Daniel Joseph Anthony Meehan (Tony Meehan) born in Hampstead.

1948

Cliff Richard comes to England with his parents, living with his grandmother in Carshalton, Surrey, first attending the Stanley Park Road primary school. Later, after eighteen months in Carshalton, the family moved to Waltham Cross, living with an aunt until a council house became available.

1951

Cliff fails his 11-plus examinations, and goes to Cheshunt Secondary Modern School. While at that school he joins a local group, The Quintones, and then later the Dick Teague Skiffle Group, where he meets Terry Smart.

1954

Appears in public for the first time at a Youth Fellowship dance in Cheshunt.

1957

While Cliff is working as a credit control clerk in the Ferguson's radio and television factory in Enfield, where his father is also employed, up in Newcastle Hank Marvin has joined his first group, the Crescent City Skiffle Group – playing banjo.

1958

Up in Newcastle, Hank Marvin has now teamed up with Bruce Welch, who was in another skiffle group, the Railroaders. They had first met at grammar school. Early in 1958 the Railroaders make three trips to London to take part in talent competition at Edmonton Regal.

6 April. In the finals of the talent show, the Railroaders come third – beaten by a Malayan opera singer and a jazz band. Hank and Bruce stay down in London, even though their group breaks up. With Pete Chester, they form the Chesternuts, releasing 'Teenage Love' on Columbia – but it flops.

During 1958, Hank and Bruce appear regularly at the 21's in Soho – where Cliff also appeared over Easter backed by Terry Smart on drums, Norman Mitcham on rhythm guitar and Ian Samwell on guitar.

Cliff also auditions for Carroll Levis, and for £6 makes a private recording of 'Lawdy Miss Clawdy' and 'Great Balls Of Fire', which he sends to Norrie Paramor at Columbia. Paramor offers him a proper recording test.

August. Cliff and his backing group begin four week season at Butlin's holiday camp, Clacton-on-Sea. His first single 'Move It'/'Schoolboy Crush' is released on Columbia, sells over 250,000 copies – winning him his first silver disc.

9 August. Cliff signs long-term recording contract with Columbia.

13 September. Cliff makes his television debut on 'Oh Boy!' (ABC TV), and subsequently becomes resident on this series.

26 September. Cliff enters the charts for the first time at Number 28 with 'Move It'.

5 October. Cliff begins tour with Kalin Twins at Victoria Hall, Hanley. For the first time Hank Marvin and Bruce Welch are in his backing group, The Drifters – recruited down at the 21's by one of Cliff's earliest managers, John Foster. The Most Brothers were on that same tour – with Jet Harris in their group. The Drifters also included Terry Smart and Ian Samwell.

25 October. Cliff makes his radio debut on 'Saturday Club' (BBC Light Programme).

November. Cliff's second single is released 'High Class Baby'/ 'My Feet Hit The Ground' (Columbia).

17 November. Cliff makes his variety debut at the Metropolitan, Edgware Road, London.

December. Hank and Bruce become permanent members of The Drifters. Jet Harris joins when Sammy Samwell decides to concentrate on songwriting, and when Terry Smart leaves to join the Navy, Tony Meehan takes his place.

1959

January. Cliff makes his first appearance with the new Drifters (who later changed their name to The Shadows) at the Free Trade Hall, Manchester.

His third single is released – 'Livin' Lovin' Doll'/ 'Steady With You' (Columbia). This was the first time the group had played with him on a recording, and they also released a single of their own 'Feeling Fine', written by Samwell, coupled with 'Don't Be A Fool With Love', but this flopped.

February. Cliff wins the Best New Singer award in the annual readers' poll organised by the *New Musical Express.*

April. Cliff's fourth single released – 'Mean Streak'/'Never Mind' (Columbia).

April. Columbia also release his first album, 'Cliff', containing these tracks: 'Apron Strings', 'My Babe', 'Down The Line', 'I Got A Feeling', 'Jet Black', 'Baby, I Don't Care', 'Donna', 'Move It', 'Ready Teddy', 'Too Much', 'Don't Bug Me Baby', 'Driftin'', 'That'll Be The Day', 'Be-bop-a-lula', 'Danny' and 'Whole Lotta Shakin' Goin' On'.

May. Appears in the film 'Serious Charge' with Anthony Quayle, Andrew Ray and Sarah Churchill.

Columbia release the 'Serious Charge' EP, on which Cliff sings 'Living Doll', 'No Turning Back', 'Mad About You' and The Drifters play 'Chinchilla'.

13 June. Jet Harris marries wife Carol Ann at St Paul's Church, Hounslow Heath.

June. Columbia release 'Cliff (Number One)' EP, featuring 'Apron Strings', 'My Babe', 'Down The Line', 'I Gotta Feeling', 'Baby I Don't Care' and 'Jet Black' by The Drifters.

July. Columbia release Cliff's fifth single 'Living Doll'/'Apron Strings' – which wins him his first Gold Disc for over 1,000,000 sales in Britain alone.

July. Columbia release 'Cliff Number Two' EP, featuring 'Donna', 'Move It', 'Ready Teddy', 'Too Much', 'Don't Bug Me Baby' and 'Driftin'' by The Drifters.

The Drifters release their second single 'Jet Black'/'Driftin'', two numbers they had featured on the 'Cliff' LP. This is not a hit – though 'Jet Black' was also released in the US with the group calling themselves The Four Jets, to avoid confusion with the American vocal group, The Drifters.

September/October. Cliff films 'Expresso Bongo' with Laurence Harvey, Yolande Donlan and Sylvia Syms. Val Guest produced and directed the film which was scripted by Wolf Mankowitz.

October. Columbia release Cliff's sixth single 'Travellin' Light'

/'Dynamite' – the first disc on which the backing group was called The Shadows. This single won a silver disc for British sales of over 250,000.

October. Cliff and The Shadows make their first appearances overseas – in Scandinavia. Tony Meehan is in hospital for an appendix operation and has to miss the trip. Laurie Joseph takes his place.

November. Columbia release the 'Cliff Sings' LP, featuring these tracks: 'Blue Suede Shoes', 'The Snake and the Bookworm', 'I Gotta Know', 'Here Comes Summer', 'I'll String Along With You', 'Embraceable You', 'As Time Goes By', 'The Touch Of Your Lips', 'Twenty Flight Rock', 'Pointed Toe Shoes', 'Mean Woman Blues', 'I'm Walking', 'I Don't Know Why', 'Little Things Mean A Lot', 'Somewhere Along The Way' and 'That's My Desire'.

December. Cliff and The Shadows appear in the pantomime 'Babes In The Wood' at the Stockton Globe.

1960

January. Columbia release 'Expresso Bongo' EP, featuring 'Love', 'A Voice In The Wilderness', 'The Shrine On The Second Floor' and 'Bongo Blues' by The Shadows.

January. Columbia release Cliff's single 'A Voice In The Wilderness'/'Don't Be Mad At Me', which earns him a silver disc for 250,000-plus British sales.

January. Cliff and The Shadows begin a six-week American tour with Freddie Cannon topping the bill. Also in the package are Bobby Rydell, Sammy 'Lavender Blue' Turner and Johnny and the Hurricanes. In New York, Cliff appears on Pat Boone's US TV show.

February. Cliff wins the Top British Male Singer award in the annual *New Musical Express* readers' poll.

February. Columbia release the 'Cliff Sings (Number One)' EP, featuring 'Here Comes Summer', 'I Gotta Know', 'Blue Suede Shoes' and 'The Snake and the Bookworm'.

March. Columbia release the 'Cliff Sings (Number Two)' EP, featuring 'Twenty Flight Rock', 'Pointed Toe Shoes',

'Mean Woman Blues' and 'I'm Walkin' '.

March. Columbia release Cliff's eighth single 'Fall In Love With You'/'Willie and the Hand Jive', which earns a silver disc for 250,000-plus British sales.

April. Columbia release 'Cliff Sings (Number Three) EP, featuring 'I'll String Along With You', 'Embraceable You', 'As Time Goes By' and 'The Touch Of Your Lips'.

June. Columbia release Cliff's ninth single 'Please Don't Tease'/'Where Is My Heart', which earns a silver disc for 250,000-plus British sales.

June–December. Cliff Richard and The Shadows appear in 'Stars In Your Eyes' at the London Palladium with Russ Conway, Joan Regan and Edmund Hockridge.

July. The Shadows have their first instrumental hit 'Apache'/ 'Quartermaster's Stores' – which is also a hit in South Africa, Spain, Rhodesia, New Zealand, Australia, India and Hong Kong.

September. Columbia release Cliff's tenth single 'Nine Times Out Of Ten'/'Thinking Of Our Love', which earns a silver disc for 250,000-plus British sales.

September Columbia release 'Cliff Sings (Number Four)' EP, featuring 'I Don't Know Why (I Just Do)', 'Little Things Mean A Lot', 'Somewhere Along The Way' and 'That's My Desire'.

October. Columbia release the 'Me and My Shadows' LP, featuring 'I'm Gonna Get You', 'You And I', 'I Cannot Find A True Love', 'Evergreen Tree', 'She's Gone', 'Left Out Again', 'You're Just The One To Do It', 'Lamp Of Love', 'Choppin' 'n' Changin' ', 'We Have It Made', 'Tell Me', 'Gee Whiz It's You', 'I Love You So', 'I'm Willing To Learn', 'I Don't Know' and 'Working After School'.

December. Columbia release 'Cliff's Silver Discs' EP, 'Please Don't Tease', 'Fall In Love With You', 'Nine Times Out Of Ten' and 'Travellin' Light'.

December. Columbia release Cliff's eleventh single 'I Love You'/'D In Love', which earns a silver disc for 250,000-plus British sales.

December. Hank Marvin secretly marries his first wife Beryl.

1961

February. Columbia release Cliff's twelfth single 'Theme For A Dream'/'Mumblin' Mosie', which earns a silver disc for 250,000-plus British sales.

February. Jet Harris's wife Carol given special leave by the High Court to present divorce petition within statutory period of three years from the date of their marriage.

February. Columbia release 'Me and My Shadows (Number One)' EP, featuring 'I'm Gonna Get You', 'You and I', 'I Cannot Find A True Love', 'Evergreen Tree' and 'She's Gone'.

February. Cliff wins Top British Male Singer award in annual readers' poll organised by *New Musical Express.*

March. Peter Gormley becomes Cliff Richard's manager, a relationship that continues to this day.

March. Cliff and The Shadows tour South Africa and later Australia and New Zealand, returning via Singapore and Malaya.

March. Columbia release 'Me and My Shadows (Number Two)' EP, featuring 'Left Out Again', 'You're Just The One To Do It', 'Lamp of Love', 'Choppin' 'n' Changin'' and 'We Have It Made'.

April. Columbia release 'Me and My Shadows (Number Three)' EP, featuring 'Tell Me', 'Gee Whiz It's You', 'I'm Willing To Learn', 'I Love You So' and 'I Don't Know'.

May. Columbia release the 'Listen To Cliff' LP, featuring 'What'd I Say', 'Blue Moon', 'True Love Will Come To You', 'Lover', 'Unchained Melody', 'Idle Gossip', 'First Lesson In Love', 'Almost Like Being In Love', 'Beat Out Dat Rhythm On A Drum', 'Memories Linger On', 'Temptation', 'I Live For You', 'Sentimental Journey', 'I Want You To Know', 'We Kiss In A Shadow' and 'It's You'.

May. Cliff's father dies due to a weak heart. Some years later Cliff was to tell the *Daily Telegraph* magazine: 'I admired him, but until about the time of his death we were never very close. When he was very ill we got on better. I suppose I looked stronger to him.'

June. Columbia release Cliff's thirteenth single 'A Girl Like You'/'Now's The Time To Fall In Love', which earned a silver disc for 250,000-plus British sales.

August. Columbia released overseas an export single 'Gee Whiz It's You'/'I Cannot Find A True Love'. So many copies were imported into this country that it became a British chart entry – Cliff's fourteenth hit single.

28 August. Cliff Richard and The Shadows open a six-week season show at the Blackpool Opera House.

14 October. Columbia release the '21 Today' album on his birthday. Tracks: 'Happy Birthday To You' (sung by The Shadows), 'Forty Days', 'Catch Me', 'How Wonderful To Know', 'Tough Enough', 'Fifty Tears For Every Kiss', 'The Night Is So Lonely', 'Poor Boy', 'Y Arriva', 'Outsider', 'Tea For Two', 'To Prove My Love For You', 'Without You', 'A Mighty Lonely Man', 'My Blue Heaven' and 'Shame On You'.

October. Columbia release the 'Listen to Cliff (Number One)' EP, featuring 'What'd I Say', 'True Love Will Come To You', 'Blue Moon' and 'Lover'.

October. Columbia release Cliff's fifteenth single 'When The Girl In Your Arms Is The Girl In Your Heart'/'Got A Funny Feeling' which earns a silver disc for 250,000–plus British sales.

October. Tony Meehan leaves The Shadows and is replaced by Brian Bennett, who was formerly with Marty Wilde's Wilde Cats. Meehan joins the artistes-and-repertoire staff at Decca.

October/November. Cliff and The Shadows tour Australia.

November. Columbia release 'Dream' EP, featuring 'Dream', 'All I Do Is Dream Of You', 'I'll See You In My Dreams' and 'When I Grow Too Old To Dream'.

November. Shadows appear at the Paris Olympia with Chubby Checker.

December. Cliff wins the Variety Club of Great Britain Show Business Personality of the Year Award.

December. Columbia release the album of music from his film with The Shadows, 'The Young Ones'. Tracks: 'Friday Night', 'Got A Funny Feeling', 'Peace Pipe' (The Shadows), 'Nothing's Impossible', 'The Young Ones',

'All For One', 'Lessons In Love', 'No-one For Me But Nicky' (Grazina Frame), 'What Do You Know, We've Got A Show and Vaudeville Routine', 'When The Girl In Your Arms Is The Girl In Your Heart', 'Just Dance', 'Mood Mambo' (The A.B.S. Orchestra), 'The Savage' (The Shadows) and 'We Say Yeah'.

December. Columbia release 'Listen to Cliff (Number Two)' EP, featuring 'Unchained Melody', 'First Lesson In Love', 'Idle Gossip', 'Almost Like Being In Love' and 'Beat Out Dat Rhythm On A Drum'.

24 December. Cliff attends the opening of 'The Young Ones' in South Africa – taking his mother and sister with him for a holiday.

1962

January. Cliff is astonished by reports that a 17 years old girl Valerie Stratford says she is going to marry him. 'It's crazy,' he says.

January. Columbia release Cliff's sixteenth single 'The Young Ones'/'We Say Yeah', which earns him a gold disc for 1,000,000-plus sales in Britain alone.

February. Columbia release 'Cliff's Hit Parade' EP, featuring 'I Love You', 'Theme For A Dream', 'A Girl Like You', 'When The Girl In Your Arms Is The Girl In Your Heart'.

February. Cliff wins the Top British Male Singer award in the annual readers' poll organised by the *New Musical Express*.

March. Cliff and The Shadows meet Princess Margaret and Lord Snowdon at the Eton College Mission's Youth Club in Hackney.

April. Columbia release 'Cliff Richard (Number One)' EP, featuring 'Forty Days', 'Catch Me', 'How Wonderful To Know' and 'Tough Enough'.

13 April. With 'Apache', The Shadows become the first British group to win a Gold Disc, and Cliff receives one for sales of 'The Young Ones'. Both are presented during a telerecording of the TV show 'Thank Your Lucky Stars'.

15 April. Jet Harris makes his last appearance with Cliff

Richard and The Shadows in the annual *New Musical Express* Poll Winners' Concert at Wembley.

22 April. Brian 'Licorice' Locking makes his first appearance with The Shadows during their concert with Cliff in Blackpool. During the same performance Bruce Welch collapses on stage and is later found to have a septic throat. He is temporarily replaced by Peter Carter when Cliff and The Shadows appear in variety in Liverpool for a week.

27 April. Announced that Jet Harris has signed a recording contract with Decca.

5 May. The Shadows and Cliff Richard seen receiving their gold discs when 'Thank Your Lucky Stars' is broadcast.

May. Columbia release 'Hits From "The Young Ones"' EP, featuring 'The Young Ones', 'Got A Funny Feeling', 'Lessons In Love' and 'We Say Yeah'.

May/June. Cliff Richard and The Shadows film 'Summer Holiday' in Greece.

May. Columbia release Cliff's seventeenth single 'I'm Looking Out The Window'/'Do You Want To Dance?', which earns him a silver disc for 250,000-plus British sales.

June. Columbia release 'Cliff Richard (Number Two)' EP, featuring 'Fifty Tears For Every Kiss', 'The Night Is So Lonely', 'Poor Boy' and 'Y'arriva'.

July/August. Cliff and The Shadows appear in the summer show 'Holiday Carnival' at Blackpool ABC.

August. Jet Harris releases his first solo single 'Main Title Theme'/'Some People', makes his solo TV debut on 'Spot The Tune' (Granada TV), and his theatre debut at the Princess Theatre, Torquay.

August. Columbia release eighteenth Cliff single 'It'll Be Me'/ 'Since I Lost You', which earns him a silver disc for 250,000-plus British sales.

October. Columbia release the LP '32 Minutes and 17 Seconds with Cliff Richard'. Tracks: 'It'll Be Me', 'So I've Been Told', 'How Long Is Forever', 'I'm Walkin' The Blues', 'Turn Around', 'Blueberry Hill', 'Let's Make A Memory', 'When My Dreamboat Comes Home', 'I'm On My Way', 'Spanish Harlem', 'You Don't Know',

'Falling In Love With Love', 'Who Are We To Say' and 'I Wake Up Cryin' '.

19 November. Records 'Bachelor Boy', which Cliff Richard wrote with Bruce Welch of The Shadows.

25 November. Appears with The Shadows on 'Sunday Night At The London Palladium' (ATV).

30 November. Columbia releases 'The Next Time'/'Bachelor Boy', his nineteenth single, earning him this third gold disc for British sales alone.

November. Columbia release 'Cliff's Hits' EP, featuring 'It'll Be Me', 'Since I Lost You', 'I'm Looking Out The Window', 'Do You Want To Dance'.

28 December. Reported that 'The Next Time'/'Bachelor Boy' has sold 250,000 copies in one week.

1963

January. Shadows enter the charts at Number one with 'Dance On'.

January. Columbia release 'Summer Holiday' LP. Tracks: 'Seven Days To A Holiday', 'Summer Holiday', 'Let Us Take You For A Ride', 'Les Girls' (The Shadows), 'Round and Round' (The Shadows), 'Foot Tapper' (The Shadows), 'Stranger In Town', 'Orlando's Mime' (ABS Orchestra), 'Bachelor Boy', 'A Swingin' Affair', 'Really Waiting', 'All At Once', 'Dancing Shoes', 'Yugoslav Wedding' (ABS Orchestra), 'The Next Time' and 'Big News'.

10 January. 'Summer Holiday' film premiere at the Warner Theatre, London – with a simultaneous premiere in South Africa.

16 January. Cliff and The Shadows begin their South African tour in Cape Town and afterwards visit Port Elizabeth, East London, Durban, Johannesburg before appearing in concert at Bulawayo and Salisbury in Rhodesia.

8 February. Reported that 'The Next Time'/'Bachelor Boy' has now passed 1,000,000 in sales and is also a hit in Norway, New Zealand, Denmark and Hong Kong.

11 February. Cliff and The Shadows appear at a charity concert in Nairobi organised by the Kenyan leader Tom Mboya.

15 February. Columbia release Cliff's twentieth single 'Summer Holiday'/'Dancing Shoes', which earns a silver disc for 250,000-plus British sales.

22 February. After being attacked in the *Daily Express* for talking on South African racial affairs, Cliff says: 'I agree that I'm not qualified to talk about it. We didn't go to South Africa to delve into the racial question. We went there to perform and entertain . . .'

23 February. Cliff Richard and The Shadows begin a six-week British tour at the Cardiff Sophia Gardens.

March. Columbia release 'Time for Cliff and The Shadows' EP. Tracks: 'So I've Been Told', 'I'm Walkin' The Blues', 'When My Dreamboat Comes Home' and 'Blueberry Hill' and 'You Don't Know'.

12 April. Cliff and The Shadows begin Scandinavian tour.

21 April. Appear at annual *New Musical Express* poll winners' concert at Wembley.

22 April. Cliff records his own BBC TV special.

May. Columbia release 'Holiday Carnival' EP. Tracks: 'Carnival', 'Moonlight Bay', 'Some Of These Days' and 'For You, For Me'.

May. Cliff holidays in Spain, where he also records, before starting rehearsals for summer show.

May. Columbia release Cliff's twenty-first single 'Lucky Lips'/'I Wonder', which earns him a gold disc for world sales.

1 June. Cliff and The Shadows open in summer show at Blackpool ABC with Carole Grey, Arthur Worsley and Dailey and Wayne (16-week season show).

June. Columbia release 'Hits From "Summer Holiday"' EP, featuring 'The Next Time', 'Summer Holiday', 'Dancing Shoes' and 'Bachelor Boy'.

July. Columbia release 'Cliff's Hit Album', featuring 'Move It', 'Living Doll', 'Travellin' Light', 'A Voice In The Wilderness', 'Fall In Love With You', 'Please Don't Tease', 'Nine Times Out Of Ten', 'I Love', 'Theme For A Dream', 'A Girl Like You', 'When The Girl In Your Arms Is The Girl In Your Heart', 'The Young Ones'. 'I'm Looking Out The Window' and 'Do You Want To Dance'.

August. Voted 'Most Promising Singer' by readers of the

American teenage magazine *16 Magazine*.

August. Columbia release Cliff's twenty-second single 'It's All In The Game', a revival of Tommy Edwards' 1958 hit, coupled with 'Your Eyes Tell On You'. It earns him a silver disc for 250,000-plus British sales.

19–21 August. Recording sessions in New York, followed by sessions in Nashville and Chicago.

August. Jet Harris and Tony Meehan release 'Applejack' (Decca).

September. Columbia release the 'When In Spain' LP, featuring Cliff and The Shadows on 'Perfidia', 'Amor, Amor, Amor', 'Frenesi', 'Solamente Uua Vez', 'Vaya Con Dios', 'Me Lo Dijo Adela', 'Maria No Mas', 'Tus Besos', 'Quizas, Quizas, Quizas', 'Te Quiero Dijiste', 'Cancion de Orfeo' and 'Quien Sera'.

September. Columbia release 'More Hits From "Summer Holiday"' EP, featuring 'Seven Days To A Holiday', 'Stranger In Town', 'Really Waltzing' and 'All At Once'.

4 September. Cliff returns to London after his US promotional and recording tour.

11 September. Jet Harris and Billie Davis injured in car crash when their chauffeur-driven car is in collision with a bus near Evesham.

22 September. Bruce Welch says he is leaving The Shadows after a final appearance on 'Sunday Night At The London Palladium', and says that his doctors have advised him to have a complete rest.

27 September. Cliff Richard says of his romance with dancer Jackie Irving: 'It's true I've taken Jackie out more than any other girl . . . I enjoy her company very much, but I can assure you that we've never even discussed the possibility of marriage – except, perhaps, to the contrary.'

3 October. Cliff and The Shadows begin eleven-day tour of Israel, during which he visits Nazareth.

October. Columbia release 'Cliff's Lucky Lips' EP, featuring 'It's All In The Game', 'Your Eyes Tell On You', 'Lucky Lips' and 'I Wonder'.

18 October. Reported in the *New Musical Express* that Bruce

Welch may stay with The Shadows after all. 'I am under strict medical supervision. Already my health has improved considerably. When we return from France, I am taking a three-week holiday in Barbados,' he says.

20 October. Cliff Richard appears on the Ed Sullivan TV show in New York. While he is in the States with Peter Gormley, The Shadows are appearing in concert in France.

25 October. Reported that Licorice Locking is leaving The Shadows so that he can be a more active member of his religion, the Jehovah's Witnesses – but Bruce Welch decides to stay with the group.

November. Columbia release 'Love Songs' EP, featuring 'I'm In The Mood For Love', 'Secret Love', 'Love Letters' and 'I Only Have Eyes For You'.

3 November. Licorice Locking makes his final appearance with The Shadows on 'Sunday Night At The London Palladium' (ATV), though he spends one final week in the studios with them recording the film music for 'Wonderful Life'.

8 November. Cliff says of Locking's decision: 'I admire Lick for doing what he wanted to do, even though it means losing a wonderful friend and musician . . .'

12 November. Bruce Welch leaves for Barbados and while he is away Hank Marvin moves home to Tatteridge and Brian Bennett moves into Hank's former home in Finchley.

15 November. Reported that Cliff has paid £30,000 for a six-bedroomed Tudor style mansion set in eleven acres of land at Upper Nazeing, Essex. 'It has only one bedroom more than our last place,' he says. 'We bought it a year ago and have only just moved in.'

November. Columbia release Cliff's twenty-third single 'Don't Talk To Him'/'Say You're Mine', which earns him a silver disc for British sales.

December/February. Cliff and The Shadows film 'Wonderful Life' in the Canary Islands with Susan Hampshire, Melvin Hayes, Una Stubbs, Richard O'Sullivan and Derek Bond.

1964

January. Columbia release Cliff's twenty-fourth single 'I'm The Lonely One'/'Watch What You Do With My Baby'. Cliff buys his holiday home in Albufeira, a fishing village on the Atlantic coast of Portugal. Peter Gormley, Frank Ifield and Bruce Welch all bought homes nearby.

February. Columbia release the 'When In France' EP. Tracks: 'La Mer', 'Boum', 'J'attendrai' and 'C'est Si Bon'.

8 February. Jet Harris begins a 29-venue tour at Edmonton Regal.

March/April. Cliff Richard and The Shadows tour Britain.

March. Columbia release 'Cliff Richard Sings "Don't Talk To Him"' EP. Tracks: 'Don't Talk To Him', 'Say You're Mine', 'Spanish Harlem', 'Who Are We To Say' and 'Falling In Love With Love'.

24 March. Billie Davis says that her romance with Jet Harris is now finished.

April. Columbia release Cliff's twenty-fifth single 'Constantly'/'True True Lovin'', which earns him a silver disc for 250,000-plus sales.

15 April. Hank Marvin reveals that he saved his 18 months old son Paul with the kiss of life after he had fallen into a goldfish pond.

24 April. Reported in *New Musical Express* that Cliff's agent Leslie Grade had turned down offers for Cliff to appear at Sands Hotel and the Desert Inn, Las Vegas; the Beirut Casino and the Shevron Hotel, Sydney.

May. Columbia release 'Cliff's Palladium Successes' EP. Tracks: 'I'm The Lonely One', 'Watch What You Do With My Baby', 'Perhaps, Perhaps, Perhaps' and 'Frenesi'.

5 May. Cliff begins European tour with The Shadows.

6 May. Scheveningen.

7 May. Leeuwarden and Blokker.

8 May. Liege, Belgium.

9 May. Brussels.

10 May. Antwerp.

12 May. Munich for TV show followed by concerts in Munich, Vienna and then Berlin.

19 May. Begin week at Paris Olympia.
27 May. Begin two-week Scandinavian tour.
4 June. Jet Harris divorced by wife Carol.
12 June. Cliff Richard tells the London *Evening News*: 'People think I must be a millionaire. 'I'm not. Nowhere near it. I have to ask my accountant if I can afford it before making a big purchase . . .'
June. Columbia release Cliff's twenty-sixth single 'On The Beach'/'A Matter Of Moments'.
1 July. Cliff Richard and The Shadows appear in hour-long ATV special.
2 July. Princess Alexandria and Angus Ogilvy attend premiere of 'Wonderful Life' at Leicester Square Empire, organised in aid of the National Association of Youth Clubs.
July. Columbia release 'Wonderful Life' LP. Tracks: 'Wonderful Life', 'A Girl In Every Port', 'Walkin'' (The Shadows), 'Home', 'A Little Imagination', 'On The Beach', 'In The Stars', 'We Love A Movie', 'Do You Remember', 'What've I Gotta Do', 'Theme For Young Lovers' (The Shadows), 'All Kinds Of People', 'A Matter Of Moments' and 'Youth And Experience'.
August. Appears in summer show at Great Yarmouth with The Shadows.
August. Columbia release 'Wonderful Life Number One' EP. Tracks: 'Wonderful Life', 'Do You Remember', 'What've I Gotta Do' and 'Walkin'' (The Shadows).
September. Columbia release 'A Forever Kind of Love' EP. Tracks: 'A Forever Kind Of Love', 'It's Wonderful To Be Young', 'Constantly' and 'True, True Lovin''.
October. Cliff and The Shadows tour Britain.
October. Columbia release Cliff's twenty-seventh single 'The Twelfth Of Never'/'I'm Afraid To Go Home'.
October. Columbia release 'Wonderful Life Number Two' EP. Tracks: 'A Matter Of Moments', 'A Girl In Every Port', 'A Little Imagination' and 'In The Stars'.
November. Columbia release Cliff's twenty-eighth single 'I Could Easily Fall In Love With You'/'I'm In Love With You'.
November. Shadows release 'Genie With The Light Brown Lamp' (Columbia).

November. Cliff appears in the Royal Variety Show with The Shadows.

December. Columbia release 'Hits from Wonderful Life' EP. Tracks: 'On The Beach', 'We Love A Movie', 'Home' and 'All Kinds Of People'.

December. Columbia release 'Aladdin and his Wonderful Lamp' LP. Tracks: 'Emperor Theme: Chinese Street Scene' (Norrie Paramor Orchestra), 'Me Oh My' (The Shadows), 'I Could Easily Fall In Love With You', 'Little Princess' (The Shadows), 'This Was My Special Day', 'I'm In Love With You', 'There's Gotta Be A Way', 'Ballet – Rubies, Emeralds, Sapphires, Diamonds' (Norrie Paramor Orchestra), 'Dance Of The Warriors' (Norrie Paramor Orchestra), 'Friends', 'Dragon Dance' (Norrie Paramor Orchestra), 'Genie With The Light Brown Lamp' (The Shadows), 'Make Ev'ry Day A Carnival Day', 'Widow Twankey Song' (Michael Sammes), 'I'm Feeling Oh So Lovely' (Faye Fisher), 'I've Said Too Many Things', 'Evening Comes' and 'Havin' Fun'.

22 December. Cliff and The Shadows open in 'Aladdin and his Wonderful Lamp' at the London Palladium with Cliff in the title role, Arthur Askey as Widow Twankey, Una Stubbs as Princess Balroubadour, and The Shadows as Wishy, Washy, Noshy and Toshy. The Shadows wrote all the music for the production which was staged for three and a half months.

1965

13 January. His and Frank Ifield's private companies taken over by Constellation Investments, bringing them £474,000. The *Daily Express* comments: 'Most of the money is likely to go to 24 year old Cliff Richard in a deal which almost certainly establishes him as a millionaire.'

14 January. Cliff Richard tells the *Daily Express* that when his accountant first looked at his finances five years earlier he had said: 'That's it boy, you're bankrupt. Now, he pays all my bills and I just sign for things.' Cliff says he draws weekly pocket money of £10.

February. Columbia release the 'Why Don't They Understand' EP. Tracks: 'Why Don't They Understand', 'Where The Four Winds Blow', 'The Twelfth Of Never' and 'I'm Afraid To Go Home'.

26 February. Reported that Cliff has formed his own film production company, Inter-State Films.

March. Columbia release 'Hits from Aladdin and his Wonderful Lamp' EP. Tracks: 'Havin' Fun', 'Evening Comes', 'Friends', 'I Could Easily Fall In Love With You'.

9 March. Reaches Number One in *New Musical Express* chart with 'The Minute You're Gone'/'Just Another Guy', his twenty-ninth release on the Columbia label.

10 March. Palladium pantomime ends, and Cliff flies to his home in Portugal for a holiday.

April. Columbia release the 'Cliff Richard' LP. Tracks: 'Angel', 'Sway', 'I Only Came To Say Goodbye', 'Take Special Care', 'Magic Is The Moonlight', 'House Without Windows', 'Razzle Dazzle', 'I Don't Wanna Love You', 'It's Not For Me To Say', 'You Belong To My Heart', 'Again', 'Perfidia', 'Kiss' and 'Reelin' and Rockin''.

April. Holiday on the Norfolk Broads with members of his Young Crusaders group from Finchley (which becomes an annual break for Cliff), and then returns to Portugal, where he records 27 tracks with The Shadows, including 13 in Italian for an Italian LP.

1 May. Reported in the *Daily Express* that Jet Harris and Lord Lichfield have gone into business together, managing groups, The Idols and Platform Six. 'My share of the business is only slight. My main activity will be to photograph the artists,' says Lord Lichfield.

May. Columbia release the 'Look In My Eyes, Maria' EP. Tracks: 'Look In My Eyes, Maria', 'Where Is Your Heart', 'Maria' and 'If I Give My Heart To You'.

May. Overseas Columbia release the export single 'Angel'/'Razzle Dazzle'.

18 May. Reported in *Daily Mirror*: 'Cliff Richard and Frank Ifield have made £256,000 profit on paper on the Stock Exchange in four months . . . last night Constellation hit 10s, making Cliff and Frank's shares worth £730,000.'

June. Columbia release Cliff's thirtieth single. 'On My Word'/ 'Just A Little Bit Too Late' and also The Shadows' single 'Stingray' and 'Alice In Wonderland'.

5 June. Cliff tells *Disc Weekly* that he does not know what happens to the greater part of his money. 'I leave it to the businessmen. All I've asked is that they tell me six months before I go broke so that I can get out!'

13 June. Cliff and The Shadows appear on 'Sunday Night At The London Palladium'.

June. Cliff and The Shadows record three hour-long ATV specials.

July. Columbia release 'More Hits By Cliff' LP. Tracks: 'It'll Be Me', 'The Next Time', 'Bachelor Boy', 'Summer Holiday', 'Dancing Shoes', 'Lucky Lips', 'It's All In The Game', 'Don't Talk To Him', 'I'm The Lonely One', 'Constantly', 'On The Beach', 'A Matter Of Moments', 'The Twelfth Of Never' and 'I Could Easily Fall In Love With You'.

6 July. Cliff begins a Continental tour with The Shadows, visiting Spain, France and Switzerland.

7 July. Frejus.

8 July. Vienne.

9 July. Biarritz.

10 July. Marseilles.

11 July. Valbonne.

12 July. Casablanca.

14 July. Zurich.

15 July. Colmar.

16 July. Geneva.

25 July. Cliff tells *Disc Weekly*: 'I never eat lunch, apart from something like cheese and biscuits. I don't even have breakfast or a good meal when I get home in the evening . . . I've got to look after my weight.'

26–28 July. Appears at Southend Odeon with The Shadows and Des O'Connor.

2–4 August. Appears at Bournemouth Gaumont with The Shadows and Des O'Connor.

4 August. Cliff says: 'Every time a serious film is talked about for me, someone says, "Cliff Richard's a pop singer, not and actor!" It's my biggest handicap . . . I'd love to

appear in a film with Albert Finney or Alan Bates, even a small part.'

9 August. Reported that he is Number One with 'Lucky Lips' in six countries – Norway, Israel, South Africa, Hong Kong, Sweden and Holland. The single had been released two years earlier in Britain.

10 August. Cliff is presented with his third gold disc for 'Bachelor Boy'/'The Next Time' on the 100th edition of 'Thank Your Lucky Stars' (ABC TV).

August. Columbia release the 'When In Rome' LP Tracks: 'Come Prima', 'Nel Blu Dipinto Di Blu', 'Concerto d'autumno', 'O Mio Signore', 'Maria Ninguem', 'Non L'ascoltare', 'Dicitencello Vuie', 'Arrivederci Roma', 'Carina', 'Legata Ad Un Granello Di Sabbia', 'Casa Senza Finestre', 'Che Cosa del Farai Mio Amore' and 'Per Un Bacio d'Amor'.

14 August. Cliff tells *Disc Weekly*: 'I would like to get married very much eventually . . . I've no-one particular in mind at present. There's been a couple of false alarms which I wouldn't want to happen again.'

August. Columbia release Cliff's thirty-first single 'Time In Between'/'Look Before You Love'.

2 September. Appears in charity show at Northampton ABC to raise funds for the rebuilding of Milton Keynes Church.

September. Columbia release 'Angel' EP. Tracks: 'Angel', 'I Only Came To Say Goodbye', 'On My Word' and 'The Minute You're Gone'.

15 September. First ATV special shown on ITV network.

22 September. Second ATV special shown on ITV network.

22 September. Films U.S. TV show for Ed Sullivan.

29 September Third ATV special shown on ITV network.

October. Columbia release 'Take Four' EP. Tracks : 'Boom Boom', 'My Heart Is An Open Book', 'Lies And Kisses' and 'Sweet And Gentle'.

11 October. Appears at the Roma Theatre in Warsaw – his first Polish concert. Then visits Lebanon, Switzerland and France with The Shadows.

21 October. BBC Light Programme presents 'The Cliff Richard Story'.

29 October. Columbia release Cliff's thirty-second single 'Wind

Me Up And Let Me Go'/'The Night', which earns him a silver disc.

November. Columbia release the 'Love Is Forever' LP. Tracks: 'Everyone Needs Someone To Love', 'Long Ago (And Far Away)', '(All Of A Sudden) My Heart Sings', 'Have I Told You Lately That I Love You', 'Fly Me To The Moon', 'Theme from "A Summer Place"', 'I Found A Rose', 'My Foolish Heart', 'Through The Eye Of A Needle', 'My Coloring Book', 'I'll Walk Alone', 'Someday (You'll Want Me To Want You)', 'Paradise Lost' and 'Look Homeward Angel'.

24 November. Cliff tells *Daily Express*: 'I now arrange my work to have weekends free for youth activities. All my closest friends are teachers.'

27 November. Shadows top the bill on 'Thank Your Lucky Stars' (ABC TV) – over The Beatles! 'We signed The Shadows to top the bill before we learned The Beatles would have a single out,' says an ABC TV spokesman.

December. Shadows release 'War Lord' (Columbia).

December. Cliff is appointed assistant leader of the Crusaders at his local church in Finchley.

4 December. Cliff says: 'I haven't seen Jet (Harris) for years, but I must say he's been quite a disappointment to me. When he left us, he and Tony Meehan made a couple of great records and we thought, great, there'll be some great instrumentals coming out. Such a shame.'

4 December. Appears in show at his old school, Cheshunt Secondary Modern, to raise funds for the local boys' club.

11 December. Cliff tells *Melody Maker*: 'I'd only record a protest song if it was a great song.'

18 December. Tells the London *Evening Standard* that both his sisters have become Jehovah's Witnesses. 'I can't tell you the change it has made in their lives. The confidence is ridiculous.'

December. Appears in Christmas TV show 'Once Upon A Wishbone'.

1966

1 January. Tells *Disc*: 'As far as I'm concerned, long resident

shows are out . . . seasonal shows and long provincial one-nighters spoil my social life – something I have begun to enjoy more than anything else.'

31 January. Cliff and The Shadows make their cabaret debut at the Talk of the Town, London, appearing there for four weeks.

5 February. Cliff reported to have said: 'I went out with Jackie Irving for over three years, and marriage crossed my mind then. But I couldn't see it working, and so I broke it off as discreetly as possible. That was two years ago, almost . . .'

February. Columbia release 'Wind Me Up' EP. Tracks: 'Wind Me Up (Let Me Go)', 'The Night', 'The Time In Between' and 'Look Before You Love'.

6 March. Records BBC-2 'Show of the Week', Cliff's first BBC TV show for three years.

12 March. Cliff tells *Disc Weekly* that he is planning to leave show business to become a teacher. 'I've given this a lot of thought for some time,' he says.

18 March. Columbia release Cliff's thirty-third single 'Blue Turns To Grey', written by Mick Jagger and Keith Richard of the Rolling Stones, coupled with 'Somebody Loses'.

3 April. Appears with The Shadows in Stars Organisation for Spastics Show at the Wembley Empire Pool.

April. Participates in service at the Royal Albert Hall to mark the 25th anniversary of the Lee Abbey Christian Community at the invitation of the Bishop of Coventry.

April. Columbia release 'Hits From When In Rome' EP. Tracks: 'Come Prima', 'Nel Blu Dipinto Di Blu', 'Decitencello Vuie' and 'Arrivederci Roma'.

May. Columbia release 'Kinda Latin' LP. Tracks: 'Blame It On The Bossa Nova', 'Blowin' In The Wind', 'Quiet Night Of Quiet Stars', 'Eso Beso', 'The Girl From Ipanema', 'One Note Samba', 'Fly Me To The Moon (In Other Words)', 'Our Day Will Come', 'Quando, Quando, Quando', 'Come Closer To Me', 'Meditation' and 'Concrete and Clay'.

June. Columbia release 'Love Is Forever' EP. Tracks: 'My Coloring Book', 'Fly Me To The Moon', 'Someday' and 'Everyone Needs Someone To Love'.

8 June. Jet Harris, by then working as a barman at the Tankard and Castle pub in Cheltenham, marries hotel assistant Christina Susan Speed at Cheltenham Register Office.

16 June. Cliff Richard joins Billy Graham on stage at his Earls Court Crusade, and sings gospel song 'It's No Secret'. There is an audience of 25,000 with another 5,000 waiting outside. Cliff tells the *Daily Mirror*: 'It took me a long time to pluck up enough courage to tell the world I'm a Christian.' Billy Graham says: 'I think this has a tremendous impact on young people who have listened to Cliff or seen his films. For him to stand up and say "I am a Christian" gets thousands of young people thinking.'

18 June. Cliff's mother, 45 year old Mrs Dorothy Webb, marries his 24 year old former chauffeur, Derek Bodkin. Cliff is not told until the wedding day. 'She wanted to be married quietly and this was the only way she could do it,' he tells the *Daily Mirror*. 'I can't call him Dad,' he tells the *New Musical Express*.

24 June. Reported that he is closing down his fan club which had 42,000 members before beginning a three year divinity course (Cliff later changed his mind about that).

29 June. Reported in the *Daily Express* that Cliff gave Jet Harris a wedding present of a £700 guitar, amplifiers and fuzz box so that he could get back into the music business.

1 July. The Shadows release 'A Place In The Sun'.

2 July. Reports that Cliff is plannning to retire are denied. A spokesman for his manager Peter Gormley tells the *Melody Maker*: 'Cliff will be studying in his spare time . . . he still has contracts he is committed to for many years.'

3 July. Cliff makes radio appeal to raise funds for the Westminster Homes for elderly people.

July/August. Cliff and The Shadows film 'Finders Keepers' for his own film production company at Pinewood Studios with Robert Morley, Graham Stark, Peggy Mount and Viviane Ventura.

14 July. Jet Harris releases 'My Lady' on the Fontana label. The number was written by Reg Presley of The Troggs and produced by Tony Meehan.

15 July. Columbia release Cliff's thirty-fourth single 'Visions', recorded without The Shadows though they accompanied him on the B-side 'What Will I Do (For The Love Of A Girl)', which they also wrote.

August/September. Cliff holidays in Portugal for five weeks.

20 August. Reported that Cliff has bought his mother a home at Highfield Drive, Broxbourne, Hertfordshire, and two houses in Roslyn Close in the same district for his two sisters and his aunt.

3 September. Reported that Cliff has sold 'Rookswood', his home at Nazeing, for £43,500.

12 September. Shadows appear in variety for a week without Cliff at Bournemouth Winter Gardens.

22 September. Cliff tells the London *Evening News*: 'I have always believed in God and always prayed, but that doesn't make me a Christian. Being a Christian, to me, has been a step I didn't realise I had to take . . . I know now I could live on £20 a week if I wanted to.'

October. Columbia release Cliff's thirty-fifth single 'Time Drags By'/'The La La La Song'.

9 October. Cliff tops the bill and also comperes 'Sunday Night At The London Palladium' (ATV), where he is presented with a petition organised by Mary Clifford of Islington and signed by 10,000 fans begging him not to leave music.

22 October. Shares a platform at the Royal Albert Hall with the Archbishop of York and the Bishop of Coventry, sings two gospel songs and says: 'As a Christian I feel it is my duty to take every opportunity to profess I am a Christian and that I personally was saved by Jesus Christ.'

23 October. Shadows begin week in cabaret at South Shields La Strada.

24 October. Tells *Sunday Mirror* that he has been invited to Russia, Czechoslovakia, Yugoslavia and Bulgaria. Of his trip to Warsaw, he says: 'It was as easy-going as walking along Bond Street . . . the money just about

covers expenses. But so what? I just love new exciting experiences.'

November. Columbia release 'La, La, La, La, La' EP. Tracks: 'La, La, La, La, La', 'Solitary Man', 'Things We Said Today' and 'Never Knew What Love Could Do'.

12 November. Cliff tells *Melody Maker*: 'I don't intend to sing for the rest of my life. I want to be a teacher. I've made no secret of that. But I just don't know when . . .'

13 November. Reported in *Sunday Express* that he is to be confirmed as a member of the Church of England, and has lunched at the Athenaeum with Canon Frederic Hood, Chancellor of St Paul's Cathedral.

December. Columbia release Cliff's thirty-sixth single 'In The Country'/'Finders Keepers'.

6 December. Confirmed by the Bishop of Willesden at his own church in Finchley.

7 December. Appears on the Granada TV programme 'Cinema' discussing his films and his career.

8 December. Premiere of 'Finders Keepers' at Leicester Square Odeon – he escorts Pippa Steel, with whom he is rehearsing for 'Cinderella'.

12 December. Cliff attends the premiere of the puppet film 'Thunderbirds Are Go', in which he and The Shadows are seen as puppets performing the soundtrack.

20 December. Jet Harris awarded £11,150 damages after his 1963 crash. Judge Donaldson says: 'Although he was no Beatle and possibly no Cliff Richard, he was nevertheless at the top of his profession.'

December. Opens in the London Palladium pantomime 'Cinderella' as Buttons – with The Shadows, Pippa Steel, Hugh Lloyd and Terry Scott.

23 December. Jet Harris's second wife Susan announces that she is suing him for divorce.

1967

14 January. Cliff tells the *New Musical Express*: 'I just want to be an ordinary teacher in an ordinary secondary school. I don't care if some people do think I'm a phoney; they're entitled to their opinions and if that's the way they feel, okay.'

January. Columbia release 'Cinderella' LP. Tracks: 'Welcome To Stoneybroke' (Norrie Paramor Orchestra), 'Why Wasn't I Born Rich', 'Peace And Quiet', 'The Flyder And The Spy' (The Shadows), 'Poverty', 'The Hunt', 'In The Country', 'Come Sunday', 'Dare I Love Him Like I Do' (Jackie Lee), 'If Our Dreams Came True', 'Autumn', 'The King's Place', 'Peace And Quiet' (Reprise), 'She Needs Him More Than Me' and 'Hey Doctor Man'.

January. Appearing on the 'Five To Ten' radio religious programme (BBC Light), Cliff says: 'I've found I can mix both my Christian life and my show-biz life because I treat my show-biz life as we are Biblically told, as a job that we're going to give to God.'

14 February. Voted Best Dressed Male Star by readers of *Disc and Music Echo*.

March. Columbia release Cliff's thirty-seventh single 'It's All Over'/'Why Wasn't I Born Rich?'

April. Columbia release Cliff's 'Don't Stop Me Now' LP. Tracks: 'Shout', 'One Fine Day', 'I'll Be Back', 'Heartbeat', 'I Saw Her Standing There', 'Hang On To A Dream', 'You Gotta Tell Me', 'Homeward Bound', 'Good Golly, Miss Molly', 'Don't Make Promises', 'Move It', 'Don't', 'Dizzy Miss Lizzy', 'Baby It's You', 'My Babe' and 'Save The Last Dance For Me'.

1 April. Cliff tells the *New Musical Express*: 'I've never thought of becoming a clergyman, in fact I've never given that any thought at all. I know I wouldn't be up to it.'

27 April. Cliff tells *Disc and Music Echo*: 'I want to terminate my career as soon as I can, and ideally I'd like to start teaching religious instruction in 1968 . . . when I quit I'll keep "Cliff" because I can't stand the name Harry, but I'll add "Webb" on the end because the "Richard" thing has got to go.'

29 April. Asked how they have survived so long, Hank Marvin tells *Disc and Music Echo*: 'I think we were just lucky to get in first, without riding in on the beat boom.'

May. Columbia release 'Cinderella' EP. Tracks: 'Come Sunday', 'Peace and Quiet', 'She Needs Him More Than Me' and 'Hey Doctor Man'.

May. Columbia release Shadows' single 'Maroc 7'/'Bombay Duck'.

May/June. The Shadows make ten-week tour of Spain, Majorca, Israel, Turkey, Australia, Japan, Hawaii and Las Vegas – concerts in Hong Kong are cancelled because of political unrest there.

May/June. While The Shadows are away, Cliff films 'Two A Penny' for Worldwide Pictures of Burbank, California, part of Billy Graham's evangelical movement. With all proceeds going to charity, Cliff insists on paying the £40-a-week that the actors' union Equity says he must be paid over to charity as well. Cliff wrote three songs for the film and is also seen singing 'Twist And Shout'. It was shot with a £150,000 budget and also featured Dora Bryan, Avril Angers and Geoffrey Bayldon.

June. Columbia release Cliff's thirty-eighth single 'I'll Come Running'/'I Get The Feelin''

9 July. Cliff appears with Billy Graham on the religious programme 'Looking For An Answer' (ABC TV).

July. Columbia release The Shadows' LP 'Jigsaw'.

16 July. Cliff discusses religion with Paul Jones on religious programme 'Looking for an Answer' (ABC TV).

22 July. Jet Harris tells the *Melody Maker*: 'I was used to £1,000 a week, then I was down to £9 labouring on the roads . . . it's been very hard trying to get back on the scene.'

4–6 August. The Shadows at Yugoslavia's first national song festival at Split, take ten curtain calls after what recording manager Norrie Paramor calls a 'quite fantastic' reception.

August. Cliff has three-week holiday in Portugal.

19 August. Cliff tells *Disc and Music Echo*: 'I'm very proud of my roses this year.'

September. Columbia release Cliff's thirty-ninth single 'The Day I Met Marie', written by Hank Marvin, coupled with 'Our Story Book'.

23 September. Cliff wins the Top Male Singer award in the annual *Melody Maker* poll, after losing the title to Tom

Jones the previous year – for the first time in eight years.

23 September. Cliff tell *Melody Maker* what he thinks of The Beatles and the Maharishi: 'I may be criticised for saying this, but I think they are searching along the wrong track . . . The Beatles have said they are searching for God. There's only one way to find him – that's through Jesus Christ.'

14 October. Cliff flies to Tokyo for two concerts and a TV special. Accompanied by recording manager Norrie Paramor, who conducted the Japanese orchestra.

October. Columbia release the 'Good News' LP. Tracks: 'Good News', 'It Is No Secret', 'We Shall Be Changed', '23rd Psalm (Crimond)', 'Go Where I Send Thee', 'What A Friend We Have In Jesus', 'All Glory Laud And Honour', 'Just A Closer Walk With Thee', 'The King Of Love My Shepherd Is', 'Mary, What You Gonna Name That Pretty Little Baby', 'When I Survey The Wondrous Cross', 'Take My Hand, Precious Lord', 'Get On Board Little Children' and 'May The Good Lord Bless And Keep You'.

29 October. Cliff tells congregation at Cuffley Free Church, Hertfordshire: 'People who just sleep around make the most unhappy marriages . . . pre-marital sex is unhealthy to the mind' (*Daily Mirror*).

November. Columbia release Cliff's fortieth single 'All My Love'/'Sweet Little Jesus Boy'.

11 November. German TV appearance.

November. Columbia release 'Carolsingers' EP. Tracks: 'God Rest You Merry Gentlemen', 'In The Bleak Midwinter', 'Unto Us A Boy Is Born', 'While Shepherds Watched' and 'Little Town Of Bethlehem'.

19 December. Reported that Cliff is to make his debut as a straight actor in ATV thriller 'A Matter of Diamonds', playing a young man who plans to rob a girl of a diamond necklace but finds himself falling in love with her.

December. Sends out 800 Christmas cards, featuring a spastic girl who can only move one foot – after seeing the girl,

Mary Older, at the Spastics Society's Pond Home near Beaconsfield, Bucks.

25 December. Cliff and The Shadows appear in Christmas Day presentation of 'Aladdin' (Rediffusion).

30 December. Cliff tells *New Musical Express* that he would love to play Heathcliffe in *Wuthering Heights*. 'He is one of the characters I admire most in all the books I have read,' he says.

1968

1 January. The Shadows make their first West End appearance without Cliff Richard – in cabaret at the Talk of the Town. John Rostill has nervous breakdown and is temporarily replaced by Licorice Locking. When Brian Bennett is taken ill with appendicitis, Cliff sits in on drums with Tony Meehan. Appear at Talk of the Town for three weeks.

12 January. Columbia release Hank Marvin solo single 'London's Not Too Far'.

28 January. Cliff Richard tells the *Sunday Times*: 'I've lived for years with people saying I'm a poof but I don't give a damn. My best friends know me and that's all that matters. Even before I became a Christian I wasn't going to lay chicks to prove myself . . .'

February. The Shadows appear in cabaret at Chequers, Sydney, and then tour Australia – where they meet John Farrar who was then in an Australian group, The Strangers.

February. Cliff films ATV play 'A Matter of Diamonds', produced with a budget of £12,000.

14 February. For the second year running Cliff is voted Best Dressed Male Star by readers of *Disc and Music Echo*.

5 March. Sings the six songs short-listed for the Eurovision Song Contest on the 'Cilla Black Show' (BBC-1), after featuring one song a week throughout the series.

9 March. Cliff's sister Joan Webb marries Colin Phipps at Hoddesdon. Cliff gives her away.

15 March. Columbia release Cliff's forty-first single 'Congratulations', the song chosen by 170,000 viewers as Britain's entry for the Eurovision Song Contest. It was written by

Bill Martin and Phil Coulter. Cliff records thirty different versions of the song for release in different countries. The B-side is 'High 'N' Dry'. The single earns him a gold disc for world sales.

March/April. The Shadows tour the Far East.

April. Columbia release 'Congratulations' EP. Tracks: 'Congratulations', 'Wonderful World', 'Do You Remember', 'High 'N' Dry', 'The Sound Of The Candyman's Trumpet' and 'Little Rag Doll'.

April. 'A Matter of Diamonds' networked on ITV.

3 April. Cliff says he now wears contact lenses instead of glasses.

6 April. Cliff comes second in the Eurovision Song Contest, staged at the Royal Albert Hall, London, singing 'Congratulations'. The show is televised in seventeen countries.

20 April. Reported that Hank Marvin's wife Beryl is suing him for divorce.

25 April. The Shadows begin season show at the London Palladium with Tom Jones.

26 April. Cliff appears in gospel concert with The Settlers in Stockholm.

27 April. Gospel concert with The Settlers in Rotterdam.

28 April. Gospel concert with The Settlers in Zagreb.

May. Columbia release 'Cliff In Japan' LP. Tracks: 'Shout', 'I'll Come Running', 'The Minute You're Gone', 'On The Beach', 'Hang On To A Dream', 'Spanish Harlem', 'Finders Keepers', 'Visions', 'Move It', 'Living Doll', 'La La La La La', 'Twist and Shout', 'Evergreen Tree', 'What'd I Say', 'Dynamite' and a medley of 'Let's Make A Memory', 'The Young Ones', 'Lucky Lips', 'Summer Holiday' and 'We Say Yeah'. The LP had been recorded live at his concert at the Shibuya public hall in Tokyo on October 18th, 1967.

2 May. Reported that Bruce Welch is being sued for divorce by his wife Ann, who is citing Olivia Newton-John. Welch had been married nine years and had a seven year old son.

13 May. Cliff begins four-week season at the Talk of the Town without The Shadows.

11 June. Rediffusion screen TV special 'Cliff Richard and The Shadows' to mark their tenth anniversary in the music business.

13–16 June. Because Cliff is ill with a stomach upset, The Shadows take his place at the Bratislava Song Festival in Czechoslovakia.

20 June. 'Two A Penny' premiered at the Prince Charles Cinema.

21 June. Columbia release Cliff's forty-second single 'I'll Love You Forever Today'/'Girl, You'll Be A Woman Soon'.

28 June. Cliff appears in his own one-man TV show 'Cliff Richard at the Talk of the Town' (BBC-2).

15 July. Shadows appear in cabaret for a week at Darwen Cranberry Fold Inn.

22 July. Shadows begin week at the Eccles Talk of the North.

August. Columbia release 'Two A Penny' LP. Tracks: 'Two A Penny', 'I'll Love You Forever Today', 'Questions', 'Long Is The Night' (instrumental), 'Lonely Girl', 'And Me (I'm On The Outside Now)', 'Daybreak', 'Twist And Shout', 'Celeste' (instrumental), 'Wake Up, Wake Up', 'Cloudy', 'Red Rubber Ball', 'Close To Kathy' and 'Rattler'.

10 August. Cliff tells *Disc and Music Echo*: 'When John Lennon came out with that quote about The Beatles being more popular than Jesus Christ, I regarded it as the height of childishness for a supposed adult cynic.'

10 August. Reported that The Shadows are to break up at Christmas. Brian Bennett tells *Disc and Music Echo*: 'I'm definitely leaving in December. And I think Bruce is leaving also. I've had enough myself. I've been on the road for eleven years altogether. My family is growing up now and I want to stay home.'

August/September. Cliff makes a six-week promotional trip to the U.S.

15 August. Jet Harris found slumped over the steering wheel of a stationary car, and is remanded on bail at Marlborough Street Court accused of being in charge of a car while unfit to drive through drink or drugs and of being in possession of cannabis and LSD.

14 September. Cliff's sister Jackie (20) marries landscape gar-

dener Peter Harrison (19), at Hoddesdon Register Office. Afterwards Cliff's mother says. 'All I have to do now is get Cliff married off.'

14 September. The Shadows begin a ten day tour of Denmark.

19 September. Cliff opens in 'The Autumn Show' at the London Palladium for a twelve and a half week season. The Chris Barber Band appear with him until September 30 when The Shadows join the show after their Danish tour.

September. Columbia release special album to mark Cliff and The Shadows' tenth year in the music business. 'Established 1958' with seven tracks by Cliff, seven by The Shadows, and all fourteen written by the group. Tracks: 'Don't Forget To Catch Me', 'Voyage To The Bottom Of The Bath' (The Shadows), 'Not The Way That It Should Be', 'Poem' (The Shadows), 'The Dreams I Dream', 'The Average Life Of A Daily Man' (The Shadows), 'Somewhere By The Sea', 'Banana Man' (The Shadows), 'Girl On The Bus', 'The Magical Mrs Clamps' (The Shadows), 'Ooh La La', 'Here I Go Again Loving You' (The Shadows), 'What's Behind The Eyes Of Mary', 'Maggie's Samba' (The Shadows).

September. Columbia release Cliff's forty-third single 'Marianne'/'Mr Nice'.

26 September. Jet Harris given five-month gaol sentence, suspended for three years; banned from driving for three years and fined £70 at Marlborough Street Court, London, on the motoring and drugs charges. His solicitor says it is a 'very sad case of a man who had been a top musician . . . involved as a passenger in a bad car accident . . . ever since his life has been a series of complete catastrophes, which have resulted in his becoming an alcoholic. He has tried to cure himself and has had every kind of treatment.'

November. Columbia release Cliff's forty-fourth single 'Don't Forget To Catch Me'/'What's More (I Don't Need Her)'.

14 December. Cliff's Palladium season ends – and The Shadows disband.

1969

January. Cliff begins filming a six-week religious series for Tyne Tees TV, 'Life With Johnny', with The Settlers.

February. Columbia release Cliff's forty-fifth single 'Good Times (Better Times)'/'Occasional Rain'.

9 March. Reported that Jet Harris is planning to make a comeback with a Nottingham group, Shades of Grey.

12 March. Actor Terence Edmond (PC Sweet in the BBC TV series 'Z Cars') sues his wife, dancer Carol Naylor, for divorce, citing Hank Marvin.

3 April. Cliff tells the *New Musical Express*: 'The Shadows have broken up. Hank has got a solo record out. Bruce is working here in the music publishing side. Brian is getting into production and John is playing his bass for lots of people.'

5 April. Cliff tells *Disc and Music Echo* that he now draws £15 a week – every Friday. 'I think unless you are paid in hard cash and actually see your money being spent you can lose all sense of its value . . . I don't do anything these days with the sole purpose of making money.'

8 April. Cliff tells the *Daily Express*: 'In all the films I have been in I have had to be a larger-than-life Cliff Richard. What I want is a tiny little nothing part opposite Albert Finney . . . no-one takes me seriously. I have an unfortunate image.'

April. Cliff tells me: 'I'm not rich, but before I took up Christianity my accountant arranged a pension scheme for me so that when I'm 60 I can retire on a fantastic pension . . . I'd like to go on working until I'm 60 if I can . . . ten per cent of the work I do is arranged so that the money goes into a trust fund for charities.'

17 May. Appears in BBC TV special with Cilla Black.

23 May. Columbia release Cliff's forty-sixth single 'Big Ship', written by Raymond Froggatt, coupled with 'She's Leaving You'.

June. Columbia release 'The Best Of Cliff' LP. Tracks: 'The Minute You're Gone', 'On My Word', 'The Time In Between', 'Wind Me Up (Let Me Go)', 'Blue Turns To Grey', 'Visions', 'Time Drags By', 'In The Country',

'It's All Over', 'I'll Come Running', 'The Day I Met Marie', 'All My Love', 'Congratulations' and 'Girl You'll Be A Woman Soon'.

11 June. Cliff goes to Israel for three weeks in the Holy Land making the film 'Fire In Zion' for Billy Graham's World Wide Films.

14 June. 'I think Jethro Tull are fantastic. I really do. They have so much talent, but the term "underground" still baffles me,' he tell the *New Musical Express*.

September. Columbia release Cliff's forty-seventh single 'Throw Down A Line', written by Hank Marvin, coupled with 'Reflections'.

12 September. Cliff tells *Disc and Music Echo*: 'Television still frightens me a little.'

October. Columbia release the 'Sincerely' LP. Tracks: 'In The Past', 'Always', 'Will You Love Me Tomorrow', 'You'll Want Me', 'I'm Not Getting Married', 'Time', 'For Emily Whenever I May Find Her', 'Baby I Could Be So Good At Loving You', 'Sam', 'London's Not Too Far', 'Take Action', 'Take Good Care Of Her', 'When I Find You' and 'Punch and Judy'.

October. Shadows re-form with Hank Marvin, Brian Bennett, John Rostill and Alan Hawkshaw replacing Bruce Welch. They spend a fortnight in Japan with Cliff and then tour Britain together.

November. Columbia release Cliff's forty-eighth single 'With The Eyes Of A Child'/'So Long'.

1970

January. Cliff receives an award from the Songwriters Guild of Great Britain for being the singer who has given the most outstanding service to British music during the past year.

January/March. Makes BBC-1 television series with Hank Marvin and Una Stubbs.

February. Columbia release Cliff's forty-ninth single 'The Joy Of Living' (with Hank Marvin)/'Boogatoo' (Hank Marvin)/'Leave My Woman Alone'.

May. Cliff makes his first straight acting appearance in 'Five Finger Exercise' at Bromley New Theatre, and receives eight curtain calls on his first night.

29 May. Columbia release Cliff's fiftieth single 'Goodbye Sam, Hello Samantha'/'You Never Can Tell', written by Hank Marvin.

June. Makes concert appearances in Rumania, Czechoslovakia and on TV in Berlin. Attends Bratislava Song Festival.

July. Columbia release 'Cliff Live At The Talk of the Town' LP. Tracks: 'Congratulations', 'Shout', 'All My Love', 'Ain't Nothin' But A Houseparty', 'Something Good', 'If Ever I Would Leave You', 'Girl You'll Be A Woman Soon', 'London's Not Too Far', 'The Dreams I Dream', 'The Day I Met Marie', 'La La La La La', 'A Taste Of Honey', The Lady Came From Baltimore', 'When I'm Sixty Four', 'What's More (I Don't Need Her)', 'Congratulations', 'Visions' and finale 'Congratulations'.

11 July. Cliff begins South African tour, lecturing at the invitation of the Bishop of Natal.

August. Columbia release Cliff's fifty-first single, 'I Ain't Got Time Anymore'/'Monday Comes Too Soon'.

9 August. Reported that Bruce Welch, Hank Marvin and Australian musician John Farrar are forming a trio – Marvin, Welch and Farrar.

24 August. Cliff tells *Disc and Music Echo*: 'I personally respect John Lennon for what he's trying to do for peace. He's doing what he thinks is right; in the same way that I make no secret that I'm using my career to promote Christianity. But Lennon has become a laughing stock among so many people. Before you gain respect for your views, whatever they may be, you have to get respect for yourself . . .'

September. Films BBC TV special in Scandinavia – and is delayed five hours at Copenhagen by a bomb scare.

September/October. Four week season in cabaret at the Talk of the Town, London.

October. Columbia release 'About That Man' LP, on which Cliff tells the story of Jesus in the words of the 'Living New Testament'. The songs are: 'Sweet Little Jesus Boy', 'Where Is That Man', 'Can't It Be True?' and 'Reflections'.

9 October. Receives the National Viewers and Listeners Asso-

ciation annual award for 'outstanding contribution to religious broadcasting and light entertainment'. Presented by Malcolm Muggeridge. Mrs Mary Whitehouse tells him: 'You have really made nonsense of this thing about the generation gap.'

October. Cliff tells *Melody Maker*: 'I have read what George Harrison thinks on religion and I respect him for what he is doing.'

11–14 November. British concerts.

18–21 November. British concerts.

November. Columbia release 'Tracks 'N' Grooves' LP. Tracks: 'Early In The Morning', 'As I Walk Into The Morning Of Your Life', 'Love, Truth And Emily Stone', 'My Head Goes Around', 'Put My Mind At Ease', 'Abraham, Martin And John', 'The Girl Can't Help It', 'Bang Bang (My Baby Shot Me Down)', 'I'll Make It All Up To You', 'I'd Just Be Fool Enough', 'Don't Let Tonight Ever End', 'What A Silly Thing To Do', 'Your Heart's Not In Your Love', 'Don't Ask Me To Be Friends' and 'Are You Only Fooling Me'.

November. Columbia release 'His Land' LP. Tracks: 'Ezekial's Vision' (Ralph Carmichael Orchestra), 'Dry Bones' (Ralph Carmichael Orchestra), 'His Land', 'Jerusalem, Jerusalem', 'The New 23rd', 'His Land', 'Hava Nagila' (Ralph Carmichael Orchestra), 'Over In Bethlehem' (with Cliff Barrows), 'Keep Me Where Love Is', 'He's Everything To Me' (with Cliff Barrows) and 'Narration and Hallelujah' (Cliff Barrows).

1971

8 January. Columbia release Cliff's fifty-second single 'Sunny Honey Girl', with two tracks on the B-side 'I Was Only Fooling Myself' and 'Don't Move Away' on which he sang a duet with Olivia Newton-John.

January. Begins another 13-week BBC-1 television series, 'It's Cliff Richard' with Hank Marvin. Marvin, Welch and Farrar appear on five shows. Mary Hopkin appears in the series singing the songs from which viewers select one as British entry in the Eurovision Song Contest.

February. Marvin, Welch and Farrar release their first LP, titled simply 'Marvin, Welch and Farrar'. One track 'Faithful' is released as a single (Columbia).

19 February. Hank Marvin divorced by first wife Beryl. Court told they parted in 1968. Grounds are Marvin's adultery with Carol Naylor, former wife of actor Terence Edmund.

6 March. Reported that Cliff had discussed religion at Evensong at Stanmore Baptist Church. 'He is a very sincere person who practises what he preaches. I would like to see other pop stars set the example Cliff has done,' says Reverend Patrick Goodland.

March. Columbia release Cliff's fifty-third single 'Silvery Rain'/'Annabella Umbarella'/'Time Flies'.

March. Marvin, Welch and Farrar tour Belguim, Germany and Switzerland.

10 May. Cliff appears in the play 'The Potting Shed' at the Bromley New Theatre. 'I have been looking forward to this for some time. I just wanted to get back to acting,' he tells the *New Musical Express.*

Hank marries Carol Naylor, and they move to their new home – a 53-acre estate with a 17th Century mansion at Higher Wiscombe near Southleigh, Devon.

13 June. Cliff appears in London Palladium charity concert to help dependents of singer Dickie Valentine, his pianist Sid Boatman and drummer Dave Pearson, who all died in an accident and between them left ten children. Frankie Vaughan, Labi Siffre, Olivia Newton-John and Marvin, Welch and Farrar also appear.

June. Columbia release Cliff's fifty-fourth single 'Flying Machine'/'Pigeon'.

11–30 October. Cliff appears at the London Palladium with Olivia Newton-John and Marvin, Welch and Farrar, breaking all previous attendance records at the theatre.

October. Columbia release Cliff's fifty-fifth single 'Sing A Song Of Freedom'/'A Thousand Conversations'.

30 October. 'We're not going mad with work – just doing enough to keep ourselves happy,' Bruce Welch tells *New Musical Express.*

November. Marvin, Welch and Farrar release their second LP 'Second Opinion', from which their single 'Marmaduke' is taken (Columbia).

17 November. Cliff begins a British tour at Gloucester ABC with Olivia Newton-John and Marvin, Welch and Farrar.

1972

January. Begins 13-week BBC-1 TV series 'It's Cliff Richard' with Olivia Newton-John.

February. Columbia release Cliff's fifty-sixth single 'Jesus'/ 'Mr Cloud'.

March. Cliff begins a six-month overseas schedule visiting most countries in Europe, the Far East and Israel.

July. Columbia release Cliff's fifty-seventh single 'Living In Harmony'/'Empty Chairs'.

September. Cliff begins a seven-week British tour.

November. Columbia release 'The Best of Cliff Volume 2' LP. Tracks: 'Goodbye Sam, Hello Samantha', 'Marianne', 'Throw Down A Line', 'Jesus', 'Sunny Honey Girl', 'I Ain't Got Time Anymore', 'Flying Machine', 'Sing A Song of Freedom', 'With The Eyes Of A Child', 'Good Times (Better Times)', 'I'll Love You Forever Today', 'The Joy Of Living', 'Silvery Rain' and 'Big Ship'.

December. Columbia release Cliff's fifty-eighth single 'A Brand New Song'/'The Old Accordion', which becomes his first flop in fourteen and a half years. 'I really can't understand why, because I played it to my mother and she was sure it'd be a hit,' he tells *Melody Maker*.

1973

January. Appears for six weeks on Cilla Black's BBC-1 television series, singing songs entered for the Eurovision Song Contest.

January. Begins three week season at the Talk of the Town, London.

17 February. Tells *Melody Maker*: 'Mary Whitehouse is ten years ahead of her time . . . the cinema medium is being wasted. Morally, something has got to be done about it. There's a need for censorship.'

9 March. Columbia release Cliff's fifty-ninth single 'Power To All Our Friends', the song chosen for him to sing in the Eurovision Song Contest, written by Guy Fletcher and Doug Flett, coupled with 'Come Back Billie Joe'. At the time it was widely reported to be his sixtieth single – but one of them, the export single 'Angel'/'Razzle Dazzle' (May 1965) was not issued in this country. 'Power To All Our Friends' earned Cliff a gold disc for world sales.

1 April. Cliff tells the *News of the World*: 'In the past two or three years I've not dated many girls at all. I don't know whether the inclination has gone or not . . . at the moment there's no-one I want to date . . . I've not gone out saying to myself "I'll find a virgin!" If I fell in love with a girl it wouldn't matter how promiscuous she'd been. It wouldn't worry me. That's because the fantastic thing about Christianity is it doesn't matter what you were, but what you're going to be as a Christian.'

June. Columbia release Cliff's sixtieth single 'Help It Along'/ 'The Days Of Love'/ 'Tomorrow Rising'/'Ashes to Ashes'.

1 September. Cliff joins Billy Graham and Johnny Cash on stage at religious crusade at Wembley Stadium.

November. Film 'Take Me High' shown in London. Music and lyrics by Tony Cole. With Cliff Richard in the film are Debbie Watling, Hugh Griffith and George Cole.

26 November. John Rostill is electrocuted at his home. Inquest records an open verdict.

December. Columbia release Cliff's sixty-first single 'Take Me High'/'Celestial Houses'.

December. Columbia release 'Take Me High' LP. Tracks: 'It's Only Money', 'Midnight Blue', 'Hover' (Instrumental), 'Why?' (with Anthony Andrews), 'Life', 'Driving', 'The Game', 'Brumburger Duet' (with Debbie Watling), 'Take Me High', 'The Anti-brotherhood Of Man', 'Winning', 'Driving' (instrumental), 'Join The Band', 'The World Is Love' and 'Brumburger (finale).

1974

30 January. Cliff tells the *Romford Express*: 'I give a lot (of

money) away to various charities. There's so much in this world that is wrong and I do my best personally to alleviate it.'

26 April. Columbia release Cliff's sixty-second single 'You Keep Me Hanging On'/'Love Is Here'.

Columbia release 'Help It Along' LP, recorded live at a charity concert. Tracks: 'Day By Day', 'Celestial Houses', 'Jesus', 'Silvery Rain', 'Jesus Loves You', 'Fire And Rain', 'Yesterday, Today And Forever', 'Mr Businessman', 'Help It Along', 'Amazing Grace', 'Higher Ground' and 'Sing A Song Of Freedom'.

October. Columbia release the LP 'The 31st of February Street', Cliff's first new studio album project in four years with four of his own songs – 'Nothing To Remind Me', 'Fireside Song', 'There You Go Again' and 'Our Love Could Be So Real'. Other tracks: 'Give Me Back That Old Familiar Feeling', 'The Leaving', 'Travelling Light', 'No Matter What', 'Going Away', 'A Long Long Time' and 'You Will Never Know'.

27 October. Shadows re-formed to appear with Cliff in charity concert at the London Palladium. Original members Hank Marvin, Bruce Welch and Brian Bennett are joined by John Farrar, replacing late John Rostill. Concert is to raise funds for widow of former BBC TV producer Colin Charman.

November/December. Cliff tours Britain – Birmingham (November 7), Bristol (8), Chatham (9), Caerphilly (13–16), Oxford (20–21), Southport (22–23), Portsmouth (27), Croydon (28), Eastbourne (29), Bournemouth (30), Sheffield (December 4), Leicester (5), Derby (6), St Albans (7), Manchester (11), Leeds (12), Sunderland (13) and Hull (14).

1975

January. Shadows begin TV series with Lulu singing the songs from which the entry for the Eurovision Song Contest will be chosen.

March. Shadows represent Britain in the Eurovision Song Contest, staged in Stockholm.